Table Of Contents

Introduction

I0390514

1. Box

We're still heavily into the box. We love the box. We have amazing computers today, and amazing hardware in the pipeline. I still spend a lot of my time working on new computers, and it will always be a primal thing for Apple. But the user experience is what we care about most, and we're expanding that experience beyond the box by making better use of the Internet. The user experience now entails four things: the hardware, the operating system, the applications, and the Net. We want to do all four uniquely well for our customers.

Name: Apple's One-Dollar-a-Year Man
Published in: Fortune
Date: Jan 24, 2000
Source URL:
http://money.cnn.com/magazines/fortune/fortune_archive/2000/01/24/272277/index.htm

2. Mac Price

The Mac was originally intended to be a consumer PC. One of the big arguments I had with John Sculley was that the Mac was designed to sell for $1,000. Yes, we overshot a little and it cost too much to make to sell for that, but even so, I thought it should have sold for between $1,500 and $1,799. John wanted to bump it up to $2,499. His vision was to keep on going all the way up and have Macs selling for $5,000 or $10,000. After I left, that's exactly what Apple did. By some measures, it worked. Apple made a fortune, although not as much as we're making today. What they didn't understand was that they had thrown away one of the greatest chances they'd ever get to win market share. They went for $1 billion in extra profits over four or five years when what they really should have done was tell everybody they would make 'normal' profits and go for market share.

Name: Apple's One-Dollar-a-Year Man
Published in: Fortune
Date: Jan 24, 2000
Source URL:
http://money.cnn.com/magazines/fortune/fortune_archive/2000/01/24/272277/index.htm

3. iMac

On our latest iMac, I was adamant that we get rid of the fan, because it is much more pleasant to work on a computer that doesn't drone all the time. That was not just "Steve's decision" to pull out the fan; it required an enormous engineering effort to figure out how to manage power better and do a better job of thermal conduction through the machine. That is the furthest thing from veneer. It was at the core of the product the day we started. This is what customers pay us for — to sweat all these details so it's easy and pleasant for them to use our computers. We're supposed to be really good at this. That doesn't mean we don't listen to customers, but it's hard for them to tell you what they want when they've never seen anything remotely like it. Take desktop video editing. I never got one request from someone who wanted to edit movies on his computer. Yet now that people see it, they say, "Oh my God, that's great!" I don't see enough innovation like that in our industry. My position coming back to Apple was that our industry was in a coma. It reminded me of Detroit in the '70s, when American cars were boats on wheels. That's why we have a really good chance to be a serious player again.

Name: Apple's One-Dollar-a-Year Man
Published in: Fortune
Date: Jan 24, 2000
Source URL:
http://money.cnn.com/magazines/fortune/fortune_archi
ve/2000/01/24/272277/index.htm

4. What's Next

People are always asking, "What will be the next
Macintosh?" My answer still is "I don't know and I don't
care." Everybody at Apple has been working really
hard the last two and a half years to reinvent this
company. We've made tremendous progress. My goal
has been to get Apple healthy enough so that if we do
figure out the next big thing, we can seize the
moment. Getting a company healthy doesn't happen
overnight. You have to rebuild some organizations,
clean up others that don't make sense, and build up
new engineering capabilities. Another priority was to
make Apple more entrepreneurial and startup-like. So
we immediately reorganized, drastically narrowed the
product line, and changed compensation for senior
managers so they get a lot of stock but no cash
bonuses. The upshot is that the place feels more like a
young company. We're trying to use the swiftness and
creativity in a younger-style company, and yet bring to
bear the tremendous resources of a company
the size of Apple to do large projects that you could
never handle at a startup. A startup could never

do the new iMac. Literally 2,000 people worked on it. A startup could never do Mac OS X. It's not easy at a big company either, but Apple now has the management and systems in place to get things like that done. I can't emphasize how rare that is. That's what makes Sony and Disney so special. Now when we see new things or opportunities, we can seize them. In fact, we have already seized a few, like desktop movies, wireless networking, and iTools. A creative period like this lasts only maybe a decade, but it can be a golden decade if we manage it properly.

Name: Apple's One-Dollar-a-Year Man
Published in: Fortune
Date: Jan 24, 2000
Source URL:
http://money.cnn.com/magazines/fortune/fortune_archi ve/2000/01/24/272277/index.htm

5. $1 a year

The board has made several incredibly generous offers. I have turned them all down for a few reasons. For the first year I did not want the shareholders and employees of Pixar to think their CEO was going on a camping trip over to Apple never to return. After two and a half years, I think that the management teams at Pixar and at Apple have demonstrated that we can handle this situation. That's why I dropped the "interim" from my title. I'm still called iCEO, though, because I think it's cool. Bottom line is, I didn't return to Apple to make a fortune. I've been very lucky in my life and already have one. When I was 25, my net worth was $100 million or so. I decided then that I wasn't going to let it ruin my life. There's no way you could ever spend it all, and I don't view wealth as something that validates my intelligence. I just wanted to see if we could work together to turn this thing around when the company was literally on the verge of bankruptcy. The decision to go without pay has served me well.

Name: Apple's One-Dollar-a-Year Man
Published in: Fortune
Date: Jan 24, 2000
Source URL:
http://money.cnn.com/magazines/fortune/fortune_archi
ve/2000/01/24/272277/index.htm

6. Next Generation Driving Industry

That's because it's so hard that if you don't have a passion, you'll give up. There were times in the first two years when we could have given up and sold Apple, and it probably would've died. But then, the rewarding thing isn't merely to start a company or to take it public. It's like when you're a parent. Although the birth experience is a miracle, what's truly rewarding is living with your child and helping him grow up. The problem with the Internet startup craze isn't that too many people are starting companies; it's that too many people aren't sticking with it. That's somewhat understandable, because there are many moments that are filled with despair and agony, when you have to fire people and cancel things and deal with very difficult situations.
That's when you find out who you are and what your values are. So when these people sell out, even though they get fabulously rich, they're gypping themselves out of one of the potentially most rewarding experiences of their unfolding lives. Without it, they may never know their values or how to keep their newfound wealth in perspective.

Name: Apple's One-Dollar-a-Year Man
Published in: Fortune
Date: Jan 24, 2000
Source URL:
http://money.cnn.com/magazines/fortune/fortune_archive/2000/01/24/272277/index.htm

7. Design Lesson

Look at the design of a lot of consumer products—they're really complicated surfaces. We tried make something much more holistic and simple. When you first start off trying to solve a problem, the first solutions you come up with are very complex, and most people stop there. But if you keep going, and live with the problem and peel more layers of the onion off, you can oftentimes arrive at some very elegant and simple solutions. Most people just don't put in the time or energy to get there. We believe that customers are smart, and want objects which are well thought through.

Name: Good for the Soul (Steven Levy)
Published in: Newsweek
Date: Oct 16, 2006
Source URL:
http://www.msnbc.msn.com/id/15262121/site/newswe
ek/print/1/displaymode/1098/

8. iPod

That's like saying you don't want to kiss your lover's lips because everyone has lips. It doesn't make any sense. We don't strive to appear cool. We just try to make the best products we can. And if they are cool, well, that's great.

Name: Good for the Soul (Steven Levy)
Published in: Newsweek
Date: Oct 16, 2006
Source URL:
http://www.msnbc.msn.com/id/15262121/site/newswe
ek/print/1/displaymode/1098/

9. Stop Piracy

Our core initial strategy on the store was that if you want to stop piracy, the way to stop it is by competing with it, by offering a better product at a fair price. In essence, we would make a deal with people. If they would pay a fair price, we would give them a better product and they would stop being pirates. And it worked. If we go back now and we raise prices—this is what we told the record companies last year—we will be violating that implicit deal. Many [users] will say, "I knew it all along that the music companies were gonna screw me, and now they're screwing me." And they would never buy anything from iTunes again.

Name: Good for the Soul (Steven Levy)
Published in: Newsweek
Date: Oct 16, 2006
Source URL:
http://www.msnbc.msn.com/id/15262121/site/newswe
ek/print/1/displaymode/1098/

10. Music

Who knows? But it's hard to imagine that music is not
the epicenter of the iPod, for a long, long, long, long,
long time. I was very lucky to grow up in a time when
music really mattered. It wasn't just something in the
background; it really mattered to a generation of kids
growing up. It really changed the world. I think that
music faded in importance for a while, and the iPod
has helped to bring music back into people's lives in a
really meaningful way. Music is so deep within all of us,
but it's easy to go for a day or a week or a month or a
year without really listening to music. And the iPod has
changed that for tens of millions of people, and that
makes me really happy, because I think music is good
for the soul.

Name: Good for the Soul (Steven Levy)
Published in: Newsweek
Date: Oct 16, 2006
Source URL:
http://www.msnbc.msn.com/id/15262121/site/newswe
ek/print/1/displaymode/1098/

11. Starting

We started in a garage. Woz (co-founder Stephen
Wozniak) and I both grew up in Silicon Valley. Our role
model was Hewlett-Packard (the electronics company).
And so I guess that's what we went into it thinking.
Hewlett-Packard, you know, Jobs and Wozniak. And, as
you recall, it was a very small company for a
long time. But the industry started to grow very
rapidly in the 1979-80 time frame. The Macintosh

team was what is commonly known now as entrepreneurship—only a few years before the term was coined—a group of people going in essence back to the garage, but in a large company. But again, that was a core team of 50 people. So that attracted a lot of people that really did want to work at a small company, in a way.

Name: Jobs Talks About His Rise and Fall (Gerald Lubenow and Michael Rogers)
Published in: Newsweek
Date: Sep 29, 1985
Source URL:
http://www.thedailybeast.com/newsweek/1985/09/30/jobs-talks-about-his-rise-and-fall.print.html

12. Best about it

Well, if I look at myself and ask, "What am I best at and what do I enjoy most doing?" I think what I'm best at is creating sort of new innovative products. That's what I enjoy doing. I enjoy, and I'm best working with, a small team of talented people. That's what I did with the Apple II, and that's what I did with the Macintosh. And, you know, over the summer, I've obviously had a lot of time to think about things. I had a piece of paper one day and I was writing down what were the things that I cared most about, that I was most proud of personally, about my 10 years at Apple. There's obviously the creation of the products Apple II and Macintosh. But other than that, the thing that I really cared about was helping to set up the Apple Education Foundation. I came up with this crazy idea that turned into a program called "The Kids Can't Wait," where we tried to give a computer to every school in America and ended up giving one to every school in California, about 10,000 computers. So if I put those two together, working with small teams of really talented people to create breakthrough products, and education, that's where the idea for doing what I'm doing now came from.

Name: Jobs Talks About His Rise and Fall (Gerald Lubenow and Michael Rogers)
Published in: Newsweek
Date: Sep 29, 1985
Source URL:
http://www.thedailybeast.com/newsweek/1985/09/30/jobs-talks-about-his-rise-and-fall.print.html

13. Early days of Macintosh

I was very happy in the early days of Macintosh. Really, up until very near the end. I don't think that my role in life is to run big organizations and do incremental improvements. Well, you know, I think that John felt that after the reorganization, it was important for me to not be at Apple for him to accomplish what he wanted to accomplish. And, as you know, he issued that public statement that there was no role for me there then or in the future, or in the foreseeable future. And that was about as black-and-white as you need to make things. Probably a little more black-and-white than it needed to be. And I, you know, I respect his right to make that decision.

Name: Jobs Talks About His Rise and Fall (Gerald Lubenow and Michael Rogers)
Published in: Newsweek
Date: Sep 29, 1985

14. Another Apple

Oh, yeah. Absolutely. I helped shepherd Apple from a
garage to a billion-and-a-half-dollar company.
I'm probably not the best person in the world to
shepherd it to a five- or ten-billion-dollar company,
which I think is probably its destiny. And so I haven't
got any sort of odd chip on my shoulder about
proving anything to myself or anybody else. And
remember, though the outside world looks at
success from a numerical point of view, my yardstick
might be quite different than that. My yardstick
may be how every computer that's designed from here
on out will have to be at least as good as a
Macintosh.

15. Home phone number

Well, given the background of the other feelings I was
feeling at the time, this was nothing out of the
ordinary. So I moved across the street, and I made
sure that all of the executive staff had my home

phone number. I knew that John had it, and I called the rest of them personally and made sure they
had it and told them that I wanted to be useful in any way i could, and to please call me if I could help
on anything. And they all had a, you know, a cordial phrase, but none of them ever called back. And
so I used to go into work, I'd get there and I would have one or two phone calls to perform, a little bit
of mail to look at. But ... this was in June, July ... most of the corporate-management reports stopped
flowing by my desk. A few people might see my car in the parking lot and come over and commiserate. And I
would get depressed and go home in three or four hours, really depressed. I did that a few times and I
decided that was mentally unhealthy. So I just stopped going in. You know, there was nobody really there to
miss me.

Name: Jobs Talks About His Rise and Fall (Gerald Lubenow and Michael Rogers)
Published in: Newsweek
Date: Sep 29, 1985
Source URL:
http://www.thedailybeast.com/newsweek/1985/09/30/jobs-talks-about-his-rise-and-
fall.print.html

16. Taken your Company

To me, Apple exists in the spirit of the people that work there, and the sort of philosophies and
purpose by which they go about their business. So if Apple just becomes a place where computers are
a commodity item and where the romance is gone, and where people forget that computers are the
most incredible invention that man has ever invented, then I'll feel I have lost Apple. But if I'm a

million miles away and all those people still feel those things and they're still working to make the next great personal computer, then I will feel that my genes are still in there.

Name: Jobs Talks About His Rise and Fall (Gerald Lubenow and Michael Rogers)
Published in: Newsweek
Date: Sep 29, 1985
Source URL:
http://www.thedailybeast.com/newsweek/1985/09/30/jobs-talks-about-his-rise-and-fall.print.html

17. Property Values

Sure it's changed. First of all, the valley has gotten to be a much larger place, it's contributing quite a bit now to the gross national product. And the entrepreneurship has gotten much more sophisticated. I mean if you want to start a company now, there are companies that help you start a company. What I hope they don't get stuck on is thinking that Apple is the yardstick of success. Silicon Valley still is a mecca that attracts amazing amounts of technical talent and I'm real excited about the next 10 years. Software is what will distinguish products in the next 10 years. And I think the technology for software is just starting to come into its own.

Name: Jobs Talks About His Rise and Fall (Gerald Lubenow and Michael Rogers)
Published in: Newsweek
Date: Sep 29, 1985
Source URL:
http://www.thedailybeast.com/newsweek/1985/09/30/jobs-talks-about-his-rise-and-

fall.print.html

18. Steve Jobs methodology

Steve had this perspective that always started with the user's experience; and that industrial design was an incredibly important part of that user impression. And he recruited me to Apple because he believed that the computer was eventually going to become a consumer product. That was an outrageous idea back in the early 1980's because people thought that personal computers were just smaller versions of bigger computers. That's how IBM looked at it.

BY LEANDER KAHNEY
(HTTP://WWW.CULTOFMAC.COM/AUTHOR/LEANDER-KAHNEY/) • 2:59 AM, OCTOBER 14,
2010

19. Minimalist

What makes Steve's methodology different from everyone else's is that he always believed the most important decisions you make are not the things you do – but the things that you decide not to do. He's a minimalist.

BY LEANDER KAHNEY
(HTTP://WWW.CULTOFMAC.COM/AUTHOR/LEANDER-KAHNEY/) • 2:59 AM, OCTOBER 14,
2010

20. Selection

I remember going into Steve's house and he had almost no furniture in it. He just had a picture of Einstein, whom he admired greatly, and he had a Tiffany lamp (http://en.wikipedia.org/wiki/Tiffany_lamp) and a chair and a bed. He just didn't believe in having lots of things around but he was incredibly careful in what he selected. The same thing was true with Apple. Here's someone who starts with the user experience, who believes that industrial design shouldn't be compared to what other people were doing with technology products but it should be compared to people were doing with jewelry... Go back to my lock example, and hinges and a door with beautiful brass, finely machined, mechanical devices. And I think that reflects everything that I have ever seen that Steve has touched.

BY LEANDER KAHNEY
(HTTP://WWW.CULTOFMAC.COM/AUTHOR/LEANDER-KAHNEY/) • 2:59 AM, OCTOBER 14, 2010

21. Recruitment

He was extremely charismatic and extremely compelling in getting people to join up with him and he got people to believe in his visions even before the products existed. When I met the Mac team, which eventually got to 100 people but the time I met him it was much smaller, the average age was 22.In each case, he always reached out for the very best people he could find in the field. And he personally did all the recruiting for his team. He never delegated that to anybody else.

BY LEANDER KAHNEY
(HTTP://WWW.CULTOFMAC.COM/AUTHOR/LEANDER-
KAHNEY/) • 2:59 AM, OCTOBER 14,
2010

22. Big Organization

The other thing about Steve was that he did not
respect large organizations. He felt that they were
bureaucratic and ineffective. He would basically call
them "bozos." That was his term for organizations that
he didn't respect.

BY LEANDER KAHNEY
(HTTP://WWW.CULTOFMAC.COM/AUTHOR/LEANDER-
KAHNEY/) • 2:59 AM, OCTOBER 14,
2010

23. Mac Team

The Mac team they were all in one building and they
eventually got to one hundred people. Steve had a
rule that there could never be more than one
hundred people on the Mac team. So if you wanted to
add someone you had to take someone out. And the
thinking was a typical Steve Jobs observation: "I
can't remember more than a hundred first names so I
only want to be around people that I know personally.
So if it gets bigger than a hundred people, it will
force us to go to a different organization structure
where I can't work that way. The way I like to work is
where I touch everything." Through the whole time I
knew him at Apple that's exactly how he ran his
division.

BY LEANDER KAHNEY
(HTTP://WWW.CULTOFMAC.COM/AUTHOR/LEANDER-
KAHNEY/) • 2:59 AM, OCTOBER 14,
2010

24. Organization

Steve would say: "The organization can become bigger but not the Mac team. The Macintosh was set up as a product development division — and so Apple had a central sales organization, a central back office for all the administration, legal. It had a centralized manufacturing of that sort but the actual team that was building the product, and this is true for high tech products, it doesn't take a lot of people to build a great product. Normally you will only see a handful of software engineers who are building an operating system. People think that it must be hundreds and hundreds working on an operating system. It really isn't. It's really just a small team of people. It's like an artist's workshop and Steve is the master craftsman who walks around and looks at the work and makes judgments on it and in many cases his judgments were to reject something.

BY LEANDER KAHNEY
(HTTP://WWW.CULTOFMAC.COM/AUTHOR/LEANDER-
KAHNEY/) • 2:59 AM, OCTOBER 14,
2010

25. Working

I can remember lots of evenings we would be there until 12 or 1 o'clock in the morning because the engineers usually don't show up until lunchtime and they work well into the night. And an engineer would bring Steve in and show him the latest software code that he's written. Steve would look at it and throw it back at him and say: "It's just not good enough." And he was constantly forcing people to raise their expectations of what they could do. So people were producing work that they never thought they were capable of. Largely because Steve would shift between being highly charismatic and motivating and getting them excited to feel like they are part of something insanely great. And on the other hand he would be almost merciless in terms of rejecting their work until he felt it had reached the level of perfection that was good enough to go into – in this case, the Macintosh.

BY LEANDER KAHNEY (HTTP://WWW.CULTOFMAC.COM/AUTHOR/LEANDER-KAHNEY/) • 2:59 AM, OCTOBER 14, 2010

26. Different CEO

The thing that separated Steve Jobs from other people like Bill Gates — Bill was brilliant too — but Bill was never interested in great taste. He was always interested in being able to dominate a market. He would put out whatever he had to put out there to own that space. Steve would never do that. Steve believed in perfection. Steve was willing to take extraordinary chances in trying new product areas but it was always from the vantage point of being a designer. So when I think about different kinds of CEO's — CEO's who are great leaders, CEO's who are great turnaround artists, great deal negotiators, great people motivators — but the great skill that Steve has is he's a great designer. Everything at Apple can be best understood through the lens of designing.

BY LEANDER KAHNEY (HTTP://WWW.CULTOFMAC.COM/AUTHOR/LEANDER-KAHNEY/) • 2:59 AM, OCTOBER 14, 2010

27. Admire Sony

The one that Steve admired was Sony. We used to go visit Akio Morita and he had really the same kind of high-end standards that Steve did and respect for beautiful products. I remember Akio Morita gave Steve and me each one of the first Sony Walkmans (http://en.wikipedia.org/wiki/Walkman). None of us had ever seen anything like that before because there had never been a product like that. This is 25 years ago and Steve was fascinated by it. The first thing he did with his was take it apart and he looked at every single part. How the fit and finish was done, how it was built.

BY LEANDER KAHNEY (HTTP://WWW.CULTOFMAC.COM/AUTHOR/LEANDER-KAHNEY/) • 2:59 AM, OCTOBER 14, 2010

28. Sony factories

He was fascinated by the Sony factories. We went through them. They would have different people in different colored uniforms. Some would have red uniforms, some green, some blue, depending on what their functions were. It was all carefully thought out and the factories were spotless. Those things made a huge impression on him. The Mac factory was exactly like that. They didn't have colored uniforms, but it was every bit as elegant as the early Sony factories that we saw. Steve's point of reference was Sony at the time. He really wanted to be Sony. He didn't want to be IBM. He didn't want to be Microsoft. He wanted to be Sony.

BY LEANDER KAHNEY
(HTTP://WWW.CULTOFMAC.COM/AUTHOR/LEANDER-
KAHNEY/) • 2:59 AM, OCTOBER 14,
2010

29. Open System

Steve believed that if you opened the system up people would start to make little changes and those changes would be compromises in the experience and he would not be able to deliver the kind of experience that he wanted.

BY LEANDER KAHNEY
(HTTP://WWW.CULTOFMAC.COM/AUTHOR/LEANDER-
KAHNEY/) • 2:59 AM, OCTOBER 14,
2010

30. No operating system

The original Mac really had no operating system. People keep saying, "Well why didn't we license the operating system?" The simple answer is that there wasn't one.

BY LEANDER KAHNEY (HTTP://WWW.CULTOFMAC.COM/AUTHOR/LEANDER-KAHNEY/) • 2:59 AM, OCTOBER 14, 2010

31. Research

We did some research and we discovered that when people were going to serve soft drinks to a friend in their home, if they had Coca Cola in the fridge, they would go out to the kitchen, open the fridge, take out the Coke bottle, bring it out, put it on the table and pour a glass in front of their guests.

If it was a Pepsi, they would go out in to the kitchen, take it out of the fridge, open it, and pour it in a glass in the kitchen, and only bring the glass out. The point was people were embarrassed to have someone know that they were serving Pepsi. Maybe they would think it was Coke because Coke had a better perception. It was a better necktie. Steve was fascinated by that.

We talked a lot about how perception leads reality and how if you are going to create a reality you have to be able to create the perception. We did it with something called the Pepsi generation

BY LEANDER KAHNEY (HTTP://WWW.CULTOFMAC.COM/AUTHOR/LEANDER-KAHNEY/) • 2:59 AM, OCTOBER 14,

2010

32. Apple Designers

An anecdotal story, a friend of mine was at meetings at Apple and Microsoft on the same day and this was in the last year, so this was recently. He went into the Apple meeting (he's a vendor for Apple) and when he went into the meeting at Apple as soon as the designers walked in the room, everyone stopped talking because the designers are the most respected people in the organization. Everyone knows the designers speak for Steve because they have direct reporting to him. It is only at Apple where design reports directly to the CEO.

BY LEANDER KAHNEY
(HTTP://WWW.CULTOFMAC.COM/AUTHOR/LEANDER-
KAHNEY/) • 2:59 AM, OCTOBER 14,
2010

33. Microsoft Designers

Later in the day he was at Microsoft. When he went into the Microsoft meeting, everybody was talking and then the meeting starts and no designers ever walk into the room. All the technical people are sitting there trying to add their ideas of what ought to be in the design. That's a recipe for disaster. Microsoft hires some of the smartest people in the world. They are known for their incredibly challenging test they put people through to get hired. It's not an issue of people being smart and talented. It's that design at Apple is at the highest level of the organization, led by Steve personally. Design at other companies is not there. It is buried down in the bureaucracy somewhere... In bureaucracies many people have the authority to say no, not the authority to say yes. So you end up with products with compromises. This goes back to Steve's philosophy that the most important decisions are the things you decide NOT to do, not what you decide to do. It's the minimalist thinking again.

BY LEANDER KAHNEY (HTTP://WWW.CULTOFMAC.COM/AUTHOR/LEANDER-KAHNEY/) • 2:59 AM, OCTOBER 14, 2010

34. Retail Stores

He brought one of the top retailers in the world on his board to learn about retail (Mickey Drexler (http://en.wikipedia.org/wiki/Millard_Drexler) from The Gap, who advised Jobs to build a prototype store before launch). Not only did he learn about retail, I've never been in a better store than an Apple store. It has the highest revenue per square foot of any store in the world but it's not just the revenue, it's the experience.

Apple stores are packed. You can go to the Sony center — go in the San Francisco center at the Moscone. There's nobody there. You can go into the Nokia store, they have one in New York on 57th St. There's nobody there. But other people have the stores. They have the products to look at. You can touch and feel them but you walk into an Apple store and it's just like an amazing experience. It is as much the people who are there shopping alongside you.

BY LEANDER KAHNEY (HTTP://WWW.CULTOFMAC.COM/AUTHOR/LEANDER-KAHNEY/) • 2:59 AM, OCTOBER 14,

2010

35. Advertisement

I remember one of the things we talked about, Steve used to ask me: "How did Pepsi get such great advertising?" He asked if it was the agencies that you picked? And I said what it really is. First of all you have to have an exciting product and you have to be able to present it as an opportunity to do bold advertising. But great advertising comes from great clients. The best creative people want to work for the best clients. If you are a client who doesn't appreciate great work, or a client who won't take risks and try new stuff, or a client who can't get excited about the creative, then you're the wrong kind of client.

BY LEANDER KAHNEY
(HTTP://WWW.CULTOFMAC.COM/AUTHOR/LEANDER-KAHNEY/) • 2:59 AM, OCTOBER 14,
2010

36. Simple

He's a minimalist and constantly reducing things to their simplest level. It's not simplistic. It's simplified. Steve is a systems designer. He simplifies complexity.

BY LEANDER KAHNEY
(HTTP://WWW.CULTOFMAC.COM/AUTHOR/LEANDER-KAHNEY/) • 2:59 AM, OCTOBER 14,
2010

37. Apple Logo

The Apple logo was multicolor because the Apple II was the first color computer. No one else could do color, so that's why they put the color blocks into the logo. If you wanted to print the logo in a magazine ad or on a package you could print it with four colors but Steve being Steve insisted on six colors. So whenever the Apple logo was printed, it was always printed in six colors. It added another 30 to 40 percent to the cost of everything, but that's what Steve wanted. That's what we always did. He was a perfectionist even from the early days.

BY LEANDER KAHNEY
(HTTP://WWW.CULTOFMAC.COM/AUTHOR/LEANDER-KAHNEY/) • 2:59 AM, OCTOBER 14, 2010

38. Drives

It's okay to be driven a little crazy by someone who is so consistently right. What I've learned in high tech is that there's a very, very thin line between success and failure. It's an industry where you are constantly taking risks, particularly if you're a company like Apple, which is constantly living out on the edge. Your chance of being on one side of that line or the other side of the line is about equal.

BY LEANDER KAHNEY
(HTTP://WWW.CULTOFMAC.COM/AUTHOR/LEANDER-KAHNEY/) • 2:59 AM, OCTOBER 14, 2010

39. Gerry Roche first mistake

So Intel lobbied heavily to get us to stay with them...
(but) we went with IBM and Motorola with the
PowerPC. And that was a terrible decision in hindsight.
If we could have worked with Intel, we would have
gotten onto a more commoditized component platform
for Apple, which would have made a huge difference
for Apple during the 1990s. In the 1990s, the
processors were getting powerful enough that you
could run all of your technology and software, and
that's when Microsoft took off with their Windows 3.1.

Prior to that you had to do it in software and hardware,
the way Apple did. When the processors became
powerful enough, it just became a commodity
and the software can handle all those subroutines we
had to do in hardware. So we totally missed the boat.
Intel would spend 11 billion dollars and evolve
the Intel processor to do graphics... and it was a
terrible technical decision. I wasn't technically
qualified, unfortunately, so I went along with the
recommendation.

BY LEANDER KAHNEY
(HTTP://WWW.CULTOFMAC.COM/AUTHOR/LEANDER-
KAHNEY/) • 2:59 AM, OCTOBER 14,
2010

40. Second mistake

The board decided that we ought to sell Apple. So I
was given the assignment to go off and try to sell
Apple in 1993. So I went off and tried to sell it to AT&T
to IBM and other people. We couldn't get anyone who
wanted to buy it. They

thought it was just too high risk because Microsoft and Intel were doing well then. But if I had any sense, I would have said: "Why don't we go back to the guy who created the whole thing and understands it. Why don't we go back and hire Steve to come back and run the company?"

It's so obvious looking back now that that would have been the right thing to do. We didn't do it, so I blame myself for that one. It would have saved Apple this near-death experience they had.

BY LEANDER KAHNEY (HTTP://WWW.CULTOFMAC.COM/AUTHOR/LEANDER-KAHNEY/) • 2:59 AM, OCTOBER 14, 2010

41. Newton

The Newton (http://en.wikipedia.org/wiki/Newton_(platform)) was a terrific idea, but it was too far ahead of its time. The Newton actually saved Apple from going bankrupt. Most people don't realize in order to build Newton, we had to build a new generation microprocessor. We joined together with Olivetti (http://en.wikipedia.org/wiki/Olivetti) and a man named Herman Hauser (http://en.wikipedia.org/wiki/Hermann_Hauser), who had started Acorn computer over in the U.K. out of Cambridge university. And Herman designed the ARM processor, and Apple and Olivetti funded it. Apple and Olivetti owned 47 percent of the company and Herman owned the rest. It was designed around Newton, around a world where small miniaturized devices with lots of graphics, intensive subroutines and all of that sort of stuff... when Apple got into desperate financial situation, it sold its interest in ARM for $800 million. If it had kept it, the company went on to become an $8 or $10 billion company. It's worth a lot more today. That's what gave Apple the cash to stay alive. So while Newton failed as a product, and probably burnt through $100 million, it more than made it up with the ARM processor... It's in all the products today, including Apple's products like the iPod and iPhone. It's the Intel of its day.

BY LEANDER KAHNEY (HTTP://WWW.CULTOFMAC.COM/AUTHOR/LEANDER-KAHNEY/) • 2:59 AM, OCTOBER 14, 2010

42. Steve & Edwin Land

Both of them had this ability to not invent products, but discover products. Both of them said these products have always existed – it's just that no one has ever seen them before. We were the ones who discovered them. The Polaroid camera always existed and the Macintosh always existed — it's a matter of discovery. Steve had huge admiration for Dr. Land. He was fascinated by that trip.

BY LEANDER KAHNEY (HTTP://WWW.CULTOFMAC.COM/AUTHOR/LEANDER-KAHNEY/) • 2:59 AM, OCTOBER 14, 2010

43. Ross Perot

Ross Perot came and visited Apple several times and visited the Macintosh factory. Ross was a systems thinker. He created EDS (Electronic Data Systems) and was an entrepreneur. He believed in big ideas; change the world ideas. He was another one. Akio Morita (http://en.wikipedia.org/wiki/Akio_Morita) was clearly one of his great heroes. He was an entrepreneur who built Sony and did it with great products — Steve is a products person.

BY LEANDER KAHNEY (HTTP://WWW.CULTOFMAC.COM/AUTHOR/LEANDER-KAHNEY/) • 2:59 AM, OCTOBER 14, 2010

44. Hewlett-Packard

HP was not a model for Apple. I've never heard that. HP had the "HP way," where Bill Hewitt and David Packard would wander people would leave their work out on their desk at night and they'd wonder around and look at it. So it was very open and it was an engineers company. Apple is a designers company, not an engineers company. HP was never in those days known for great design. It was known for great engineering, not great design. No, I don't remember HP being a model for Apple at all.

BY LEANDER KAHNEY (HTTP://WWW.CULTOFMAC.COM/AUTHOR/LEANDER-KAHNEY/) • 2:59 AM, OCTOBER 14, 2010

45. HP contribution

HP was the father of the walking around style of management. And HP was the father of the engineer being at the top of the hierarchy in companies.

41

Engineers are far more important than managers at Apple — and designers are at the top of the hierarchy. Even when you look at software, the best designers like Bill Atkinson, Andy Hertzfeld, Steve Capps, were called software designers, not software engineers because they were designing in software. It wasn't just that their code worked. It had to be beautiful code. People would go in and admire it. It's like a writer. People would look at someone's style. They would look at their code writing style and they were considered just beautiful geniuses at the way they wrote code or the way they designed hardware.

BY LEANDER KAHNEY (HTTP://WWW.CULTOFMAC.COM/AUTHOR/LEANDER-KAHNEY/) • 2:59 AM, OCTOBER 14, 2010

46. Computer Definition

Computers are actually pretty simple. We're sitting here on a bench in this cafe [for this part of the Interview]. Let's assume that you understood only the most rudimentary of directions and you asked how to find the rest room. I would have to describe it to you in very specific and precise instructions. I might say, "Scoot sideways two meters off the bench. Stand erect. Lift left foot. Bend left knee until it is horizontal. Extend left foot and shift weight 300 centimeters forward ..." and on and on. If you could interpret all those instructions 100 times faster than any other person in this cafe, you would appear to be a magician.

Name: Playboy Interview: Steven Jobs (David Sheff)
Published in: Playboy
Date: Feb 1985

47. Life changing

A computer is the most incredible tool we've ever seen. It can be a writing tool, a communications center, a super calculator, a planner, a filer and an artistic instrument all in one, just by being given new instructions, or software, to work from. There are no other tools that have the power and versatility of a computer. We have no idea how far it's going to go. Right now, computers make our lives easier. They do work for us in fractions of a second that would take us hours. They increase the quality of life, some of that by simply automating drudgery and some of that by broadening our possibilities. As things progress, they'll be doing more and more for us.

Name: Playboy Interview: Steven Jobs (David Sheff)
Published in: Playboy
Date: Feb 1985
Source URL:
http://www.playboy.com/magazine/playboy-interview-
steve-jobs

48. Computer Today

There are different answers for different people. In business, that question is easy to answer: You really can prepare documents much faster and at a higher quality level, and you can do many things to increase office productivity. A computer frees people from much of the menial work. Besides that, you are giving them a tool that encourages them to be creative. Remember, computers are tools. Tools help us do our work better. In education, computers are the first thing to come along since books that will sit there and interact with you endlessly, without judgment. Socratic education isn't available anymore, and computers have the potential to be a real breakthrough in the educational process when used in conjunction with enlightened teachers. We're in most schools already.

Name: Playboy Interview: Steven Jobs (David Sheff)
Published in: Playboy
Date: Feb 1985
Source URL:
http://www.playboy.com/magazine/playboy-interview-steve-jobs

49. Macintosh

It allowed you to intone your words with meaning beyond the simple linguistics. And we're in the same situation today. Some people are saying that we ought to put an IBM PC on every desk in America to improve productivity. It won't work. The special incantations you have to learn this time are "slash q-zs" and things like that. The manual for WordStar, the most popular word-processing program, is 400 pages thick. To write a novel, you have to read a novel—one that reads like a mystery to most people. They're not going to learn slash q-z any more than they're going to learn Morse code. That is what Macintosh is all about. It's the first "telephone" of our industry. And, besides that, the neatest thing about it, to me, is that the Macintosh lets you sing the way the telephone did. You don't simply communicate words, you have special print styles and the ability to draw and add pictures to express yourself.

Name: Playboy Interview: Steven Jobs (David Sheff)
Published in: Playboy
Date: Feb 1985
Source URL:
http://www.playboy.com/magazine/playboy-interview-steve-jobs

50. Mouse—a little box

If I want to tell you there is a spot on your shirt, I'm not going to do it linguistically: "There's a spot on your shirt 14 centimeters down from the collar and three centimeters to the left of your button." If you have a spot—"There!" [He points]—I'll point to it. Pointing is a metaphor we all know. We've done a lot of studies and tests on that, and it's much faster to do all kinds of functions, such as cutting and pasting, with a mouse, so it's not only easier to use but more efficient.

Name: Playboy Interview: Steven Jobs (David Sheff)
Published in: Playboy
Date: Feb 1985
Source URL:
http://www.playboy.com/magazine/playboy-interview-steve-jobs

51. Time to develop Macintosh

It was more than two years on the computer itself. We had been working on the technology behind it for years before that. I don't think I've ever worked so hard on something, but working on Macintosh was the neatest experience of my life. Almost everyone who worked on it will say that. None of us wanted to release it at the end. It was as though we knew that once it was out of our hands, it wouldn't be ours anymore. When we finally presented it at the shareholders' meeting, everyone in the auditorium stood up and gave it a five-minute ovation. What was incredible to me was that I could see the Mac team in the first few rows. It was as though none of us could believe that we'd actually finished it. Everyone started crying.

Name: Playboy Interview: Steven Jobs (David Sheff)
Published in: Playboy
Date: Feb 1985
Source URL:
http://www.playboy.com/magazine/playboy-interview-steve-jobs

52. Lisa and Apple III

If you want to try that one, add the people who bought the IBM PCs or the PCjrs to that list, too. As far as Lisa is concerned, since some of its technology was used in the Macintosh, it can now run Macintosh software and is being seen as a big brother to Macintosh; though it was unsuccessful at first, our sales of Lisa are going through the roof. We're also still selling more than 2000 Apple IIIs a month—more than half to repeat buyers. The over-all point is that new technology will not necessarily replace old technology, but it will date it. By definition. Eventually, it will replace it. But it's like people who had black-and-white TVs when color came out. They eventually decided whether or not the new technology was worth the investment.

Name: Playboy Interview: Steven Jobs (David Sheff)
Published in: Playboy
Date: Feb 1985
Source URL:
http://www.playboy.com/magazine/playboy-interview-steve-jobs

53. Apple II and IBM PC

Before Macintosh, there were two standards: Apple II and IBM PC. Those two standards are like rivers carved in the rock bed of a canyon. It's taken years to carve them—seven years to carve the Apple II and four years to carve the IBM. What we have done with Macintosh is that in less than a year, through the momentum of the revolutionary aspects of the product and through every ounce of marketing that we have as a company, we have been able to blast a third channel through that rock and make a third river, a third standard. In my opinion, there are only two companies that can do that today, Apple and IBM. Maybe that's too bad, but to do it right now is just a monumental effort, and I don't think that Apple or IBM will do that in the next three or four years. Toward the end of the Eighties, we may be seeing some new things.

Name: Playboy Interview: Steven Jobs (David Sheff)
Published in: Playboy
Date: Feb 1985
Source URL:
http://www.playboy.com/magazine/playboy-interview-steve-jobs

54. Apple near bankruptcy

No, no, no. In fact, 1983, when all these predictions were being made, was a phenomenally successful year for Apple. We virtually doubled in size in 1983. We went from $583,000,000 in 1982 to something like $980,000,000 in sales. It was almost all Apple II-related. It just didn't live up to our expectations. If Macintosh weren't a success, we probably would have stayed at something like a billion dollars a year, selling Apple IIs and versions of it.

Name: Playboy Interview: Steven Jobs (David Sheff)
Published in: Playboy
Date: Feb 1985
Source URL:
http://www.playboy.com/magazine/playboy-interview-steve-jobs

55. Lisa failure

First of all, it was too expensive—about ten grand. We had gotten Fortune 500-it is, trying to sell to those huge corporations, when our roots were selling to people. There were other problems: late shipping; the software didn't come together in the end as well as we hoped and we lost a lot of momentum. And IBM's coming on very strong, coupled with our being about six months late, coupled with the price's being too high, plus another strategic mistake we made—deciding to sell Lisa only through about 150 dealers, which was absolutely foolish on our part—meant it was a very costly mistake. We decided to hire people we thought were marketing and management experts. Not a bad idea, but unfortunately, this was such a new business that the things the so-called professionals knew were almost detriments to their success in this new way of looking at business.

Name: Playboy Interview: Steven Jobs (David Sheff)
Published in: Playboy
Date: Feb 1985
Source URL:
http://www.playboy.com/magazine/playboy-interview-steve-jobs

56. Decisions, good and bad

We tried never to have one person make all the decisions. There were three people running the company at that time: Mike Scott, Mike Markkula and myself. Now it's John Sculley [Apple's president] and myself. In the early days, if there was a disagreement, I would generally defer my judgment to some of the other people who had more experience than I had. In many cases, they were right. In some important cases, if we had gone my way, we would have done better.

Name: Playboy Interview: Steven Jobs (David Sheff)
Published in: Playboy
Date: Feb 1985
Source URL:
http://www.playboy.com/magazine/playboy-interview-steve-jobs

57. Feel losing Apple

There was a bit of that, I guess, but the thing that was harder for me was that they hired a lot of people in the Lisa group who didn't share the vision we originally had. There was a big conflict in the

Lisa group between the people who wanted, in essence, to build something like Macintosh and the people hired from Hewlett-Packard and other companies who brought with them a perspective of larger machines, corporate sales. I just decided that I was going to go off and do that myself with a small group, sort of go back to the garage, to design the Macintosh. They didn't take us very seriously. I think Scotty was just sort of humoring me.

Name: Playboy Interview: Steven Jobs (David Sheff)
Published in: Playboy
Date: Feb 1985
Source URL:
http://www.playboy.com/magazine/playboy-interview-steve-jobs

58. Difference between the people

Let me compare it with IBM. How come the Mac group produced Mac and the people at IBM produced the PCjr? We think the Mac will sell zillions, but we didn't build Mac for anybody else. We built it for ourselves. We were the group of people who were going to judge whether it was great or not. We weren't going to go out and do market research. We just wanted to build the best thing we could build. When you're a carpenter making a beautiful chest of drawers, you're not going to use a piece of plywood on the back, even though it faces the wall and nobody will ever see it. You'll know it's there, so you're going to use a beautiful piece of wood on the back. For you to sleep well at night, the aesthetic, the quality, has to be carried all the way through.

Name: Playboy Interview: Steven Jobs (David Sheff)
Published in: Playboy
Date: Feb 1985
Source URL:
http://www.playboy.com/magazine/playboy-interview-steve-jobs

59. Average age of Apple employees

It's often the same with any new, revolutionary thing. People get stuck as they get older. Our minds are sort of electrochemical computers. Your thoughts construct patterns like scaffolding in your mind. You are really etching chemical patterns. In most cases, people get stuck in those patterns, just like grooves in a record, and they never get out of them. It's a rare person who etches grooves that are other than a specific way of looking at things, a specific way of questioning things. It's rare that you see an artist in his 30s or 40s able to really contribute something amazing. Of course, there are some people who are innately curious, forever little kids in their awe of life, but they're rare.

Name: Playboy Interview: Steven Jobs (David Sheff)
Published in: Playboy
Date: Feb 1985
Source URL:
http://www.playboy.com/magazine/playboy-interview-steve-jobs

60. Beat IBM

Yes. The business market has several sectors. Rather than just thinking of the Fortune 500, which is where IBM is strongest, I like to think of the Fortune 5,000,000 or 14,000,000. There are 14,000,000 small businesses in this country. I think that the vast group of people who need to be computerized includes that large number of medium and small businesses. We're going to try to be able to bring some meaningful solutions to them in 1985.

Name: Playboy Interview: Steven Jobs (David Sheff)
Published in: Playboy
Date: Feb 1985
Source URL:
http://www.playboy.com/magazine/playboy-interview-steve-jobs

61. Benefit the consumer

That's simply untrue. Insisting that we need one standard now is like saying that they needed one standard for automobiles in 1920. There would have been no innovations such as the automatic transmission, power steering and independent suspension if they believed that. The last thing we want to do is freeze technology. With computers, Macintosh is revolutionary. There is no question that Macintosh's technology is superior to IBM's. There is a clear need for an alternative to IBM.

Name: Playboy Interview: Steven Jobs (David Sheff)
Published in: Playboy
Date: Feb 1985
Source URL:
http://www.playboy.com/magazine/playboy-interview-steve-jobs

62. Sales slipped

We've never worried about numbers. In the market place, Apple is trying to focus the spotlight on products, because products really make a difference. IBM is trying to focus the spotlight on service, support, security, mainframes and motherhood. Now, Apple's key observation three years ago was that when you're shipping 10,000,000 computers a year, even IBM does not have enough mothers to ship one with every computer. So you've got to build motherhood into the computer. And that's a big part of what Macintosh is all about. All these things show that it really is coming down to just Apple and IBM. If, for some reason, we make some giant mistakes and IBM wins, my personal feeling is that we are going to enter sort of a computer Dark Ages for about 20 years. Once IBM gains control of a market sector, they almost always stop innovation. They prevent innovation from happening.

Name: Playboy Interview: Steven Jobs (David Sheff)
Published in: Playboy
Date: Feb 1985
Source URL:
http://www.playboy.com/magazine/playboy-interview-steve-jobs

63. Software for the Apple II, can't run on Macintosh

That's right. Mac is altogether new. We knew that we could reach the early innovators with current-generation technology—Apple II, IBM PC—because they'd stay up all night learning how to use their computer. But we'd never reach the majority of people. If we were really going to get computers to tens of millions of people, we needed a technology that would make the thing radically easier to use and more powerful at the same time, so we had to make a break. We just had to do it. We wanted to make sure it was great, because it may be the last chance that any of us get to make a clean break. And I'm very happy with the way Macintosh turned out. It will prove a really solid foundation for the next ten years.

Name: Playboy Interview: Steven Jobs (David Sheff)
Published in: Playboy
Date: Feb 1985
Source URL:
http://www.playboy.com/magazine/playboy-interview-steve-jobs

64. Finding Biological parents

I think it's quite a natural curiosity for adopted people to want to understand where certain traits come from. But I'm mostly an environmentalist. I think the way you are raised and your values and most of your world view come from the experiences you had as you grew up. But some things aren't accounted for that way. I think it's quite natural to have a curiosity about it. And I did.

Name: Playboy Interview: Steven Jobs (David Sheff)
Published in: Playboy
Date: Feb 1985
Source URL:
http://www.playboy.com/magazine/playboy-interview-steve-jobs

65. Silicon Valley location

The Valley is positioned strategically between two great universities, Berkeley and Stanford. Both of those universities attract not only lots of students but very good students and ones from all over the United States. They come here and fall in love with the area and they stay here. So there is a constant influx of new, bright human resources. Before World War Two, two Stanford graduates named Bill Hewlett and Dave Packard created a very innovative electronics company—Hewlett-Packard. Then the transistor was invented in 1948 by Bell Telephone Laboratories. One of the three co inventors of the transistor, William Shockley, decided to return to his home town of Palo Alto to start a little company called Shockley Labs or something. He brought with him about a dozen of the best and brightest physicists and chemists of his day. Little by little, people started breaking off and forming competitive companies, like those flowers or weeds that scatter seeds in hundreds of directions when you blow on them. And that's why the Valley is here today.

Name: Playboy Interview: Steven Jobs (David Sheff)
Published in: Playboy
Date: Feb 1985
Source URL:
http://www.playboy.com/magazine/playboy-interview-steve-jobs

66. Hewlett-Packard

When I was 12 or 13, I wanted to build something and I needed some parts, so I picked up the phone and called Bill Hewlett—he was listed in the Palo Alto phone book. He answered the phone and he was real nice. He chatted with me for, like, 20 minutes. He didn't know me at all, but he ended up giving me some parts and he got me a job that summer working at Hewlett-Packard on the line, assembling frequency counters. Assembling may be too strong. I was putting in screws. It didn't matter; I was in heaven. I remember my first day, expressing my complete enthusiasm and bliss at being at Hewlett-Packard for the summer to my supervisor, a guy named Chris, telling him that my favorite thing in the whole world was electronics. I asked him what his favorite thing to do was and he looked at me and said, "To fuck!" [Laughs] I learned a lot that summer.

Name: Playboy Interview: Steven Jobs (David Sheff)
Published in: Playboy
Date: Feb 1985
Source URL:
http://www.playboy.com/magazine/playboy-interview-steve-jobs

67. Meeting Steve Wozniak

I met Woz when I was 13, at a friend's garage. He was about 18. He was, like, the first person I met who knew more electronics than I did at that point. We became good friends, because we shared an interest in computers and we had a sense of humor. We pulled all kinds of pranks together.

Name: Playboy Interview: Steven Jobs (David Sheff)
Published in: Playboy
Date: Feb 1985
Source URL:
http://www.playboy.com/magazine/playboy-interview-steve-jobs

68. Influence

The whole period had a huge influence. As it was clear that the Sixties were over, it was also clear that a lot of the people who had gone through the Sixties ended up not really accomplishing what they set out to accomplish, and because they had thrown their discipline to the wind, they didn't have much to fall back on. Many of my friends have ended up ingrained with the idealism of that period but also with a certain practicality, a cautiousness about ending up working behind the counter in a natural-food store when they are 45, which is what they saw happen to some of their older friends. It's not that that is bad in and of itself, but it's bad if that's not what you really wanted to do.

Name: Playboy Interview: Steven Jobs (David Sheff)
Published in: Playboy
Date: Feb 1985
Source URL:
http://www.playboy.com/magazine/playboy-interview-steve-jobs

69. Have fun and make money

Right. I decided I wanted to travel, but I was lacking the necessary funds. I came back down to get a job. I was looking in the paper and there was this ad that said, yes, "Have fun and make money." I called. It was Atari. I had never had a job before other than the one when I was a kid. By some stroke of luck, they called me up the next day and hired me.

Name: Playboy Interview: Steven Jobs (David Sheff)
Published in: Playboy
Date: Feb 1985

70. Atari's earliest stage

I was, like, employee number 40. It was a very small company. They had made Pong and two other games. My first job was helping a guy named Don work on a basketball game, which was a disaster. There was this basketball game, and somebody was working on a hockey game. They were trying to model all their games after simple field sports at that time, because Pong was such a success.

Name: Playboy Interview: Steven Jobs (David Sheff)
Published in: Playboy
Date: Feb 1985
Source URL:
http://www.playboy.com/magazine/playboy-interview-steve-jobs

71. Shaved your head

That's not quite the way it happened. I was walking around in the Himalayas and I stumbled onto this thing that turned out to be a religious festival. There was a baba, a holy man, who was the holy man of this particular festival, with his large group of followers. I could smell good food. I hadn't been fortunate enough to smell good food for a long time, so I wandered up to pay my respects and eat some lunch. For some reason, this baba, upon seeing me sitting there eating, immediately walked over to me and sat down and burst out laughing. He didn't speak much English and I spoke a little

Hindi, but he tried to carry on a conversation and he was just rolling on the ground with laughter. Then he grabbed my arm and took me up this mountain trail. It was a little funny, because here were hundreds of Indians who had traveled for thousands of miles to hang out with this guy for ten seconds and I stumble in for something to eat and he's dragging me up this mountain path. We get to the top of this mountain half an hour later and there's this little well and pond at the top of this mountain, and he dunks my head in the water and pulls out a razor from his pocket and starts to shave my head. I'm completely stunned. I'm 19 years old, in a foreign country, up in the Himalayas, and here is this bizarre Indian baba who has just dragged me away from the rest of the crowd, shaving my head atop this mountain peak. I'm still not sure why he did it.

Name: Playboy Interview: Steven Jobs (David Sheff)
Published in: Playboy
Date: Feb 1985
Source URL:
http://www.playboy.com/magazine/playboy-interview-steve-jobs

72. Apple I was for hobbyists

Completely. We sold only about 150 of them, ever. It wasn't that big a deal, but we made about $95,000 and I started to see it as a business besides something to do. Apple I was just a printed circuit board. There was no case, there was no power supply; it wasn't much of a product yet. It was just a printed circuit board. You had to go out and buy transformers for it. You had to buy your own keyboard [laughs].

Name: Playboy Interview: Steven Jobs (David Sheff)
Published in: Playboy
Date: Feb 1985
Source URL:
http://www.playboy.com/magazine/playboy-interview-
steve-jobs

73. Vision

No, not particularly. Neither of us had any idea that
this would go anywhere. Woz is motivated by
figuring things out. He concentrated more on the
engineering and proceeded to do one of his most
brilliant pieces of work, which was the disk drive,
another key engineering feat that made the Apple II
a possibility. I was trying to build the company—trying
to find out what a company was. I don't think it
would have happened without Woz and I don't think it
would have happened without me.

Name: Playboy Interview: Steven Jobs (David Sheff)
Published in: Playboy
Date: Feb 1985
Source URL:
http://www.playboy.com/magazine/playboy-interview-
steve-jobs

74. Partnership

The main thing was that Woz was never really
interested in Apple as a company. He was just sort of
interested in getting the Apple II on a printed circuit
board so he could have one and be able to carry
it to his computer club without having the wires break
on the way. He had done that and decided to
go on to other things. He had other ideas.

Name: Playboy Interview: Steven Jobs (David Sheff)
Published in: Playboy
Date: Feb 1985
Source URL:
http://www.playboy.com/magazine/playboy-interview-steve-jobs

75. Create the Apple II

It wasn't just us. We brought in other people. Wozniak still did the logic of the Apple II, which certainly is a large part of it, but there were some other key parts. The power supply was really a key. The case was really a key. The real jump with the Apple II was that it was a finished product. It was the first computer that you could buy that wasn't a kit. It was fully assembled and had its own case and its own keyboard, and you could really sit down and start to use it. And that was the breakthrough of the Apple II: that it looked like a real product.

Name: Playboy Interview: Steven Jobs (David Sheff)
Published in: Playboy
Date: Feb 1985
Source URL:
http://www.playboy.com/magazine/playboy-interview-steve-jobs

76. Rival, A.T.&T

A.T.&T.. is absolutely going to be in the business. There is a major transformation in the company that's taking place right now. A.T.&T. is changing from a subsidized and regulated service-oriented company to a free-market, competitive-marketing technology company. A.T.&T.'s products per se have never been of the highest quality. All you have to do is go look at their telephones. They're somewhat of an embarrassment. But they do possess great technology in their research labs. Their challenge is to learn how to commercialize that technology. Also, they have to learn about consumer marketing. I think that they will do both of those things, but it's going to take them years.

Name: Playboy Interview: Steven Jobs (David Sheff)
Published in: Playboy
Date: Feb 1985
Source URL:
http://www.playboy.com/magazine/playboy-interview-steve-jobs

77. Radio Shack

Radio Shack is totally out of the picture. They have missed the boat. Radio Shack tried to squeeze the computer into their model of retailing, which in my opinion often meant selling second-rate products or low-end products in a surplus-store environment. The sophistication of the computer buyer passed Radio Shack by without their really realizing it. Their market shares dropped through the floor. I don't anticipate that they're going to recover and again become a major player.

Name: Playboy Interview: Steven Jobs (David Sheff)
Published in: Playboy
Date: Feb 1985
Source URL:
http://www.playboy.com/magazine/playboy-interview-steve-jobs

78. Xerox

Xerox is out of the business. T.I. is doing nowhere near their expectations. As to some of the others, the large companies, like DEC and Wang, can sell to their installed bases. They can sell personal computers as advanced terminals, but that business is going to dwindle.

Name: Playboy Interview: Steven Jobs (David Sheff)
Published in: Playboy
Date: Feb 1985
Source URL:
http://www.playboy.com/magazine/playboy-interview-steve-jobs

79. Smaller portables

They are OK if you're a reporter and trying to take notes on the run. But for the average person, they're really not that useful, and there's not all that software for them, either. By the time you get your software done, a new one comes out with a slightly bigger display and your software is obsolete. So nobody is writing any software for them. Wait till we do it—the power of a Macintosh in something the size of a book!

Name: Playboy Interview: Steven Jobs (David Sheff)
Published in: Playboy
Date: Feb 1985
Source URL:
http://www.playboy.com/magazine/playboy-interview-steve-jobs

80. American semiconductor companies

Japan's very interesting. Some people think it copies things. I don't think that anymore. I think what they do is reinvent things. They will get something that's already been invented and study it until they thoroughly understand it. In some cases, they understand it better than the original inventor. Out of that understanding, they will reinvent it in a more refined second-generation version. That strategy works only when what they're working with isn't changing very much—the stereo industry and the automobile industry are two examples. When the target is moving quickly, they find it very difficult, because that reinvention cycle takes a few years. As long as the definition of what a personal computer is keeps changing at the rate that it is, they will have a very hard time. Once the rate of change slows down, the Japanese will bring all of their strengths to bear on this market, because they absolutely want to dominate the computer business; there's no question about that. They see that as a national priority. We think that in four to five years, the Japanese will finally figure out how to build a decent computer. And if we're going to keep this industry one in which America leads, we have four years to become world-class manufacturers. Our manufacturing technology has to equal or surpass that of the Japanese.

Name: Playboy Interview: Steven Jobs (David Sheff)
Published in: Playboy
Date: Feb 1985
Source URL:
http://www.playboy.com/magazine/playboy-interview-steve-jobs

81. Software revolutionary changes

Certainly, the earlier programming, getting a programming language on a microprocessor chip, was a real breakthrough. VisiCalc was a breakthrough, because that was the first real use of computers in business, where business people could see tangible benefits of using one. Before that, you had to program your own applications, and the number of people who want to program is a small fraction— one percent. Coupled with VisiCalc, the ability to graph things, graph information, was important, and so was Lotus.

Name: Playboy Interview: Steven Jobs (David Sheff)
Published in: Playboy
Date: Feb 1985
Source URL:
http://www.playboy.com/magazine/playboy-interview-steve-jobs

82. Word processing

You're right, I should have listed word processing after VisiCalc. Word processing is the most universally needed application and one of the easiest to understand. It's probably the first use to which most people put their personal computer. There were word processors before personal computers, but a word processor on a personal computer was more of an economic breakthrough, while there was never any form of VisiCalc before the personal computer.

Name: Playboy Interview: Steven Jobs (David Sheff)
Published in: Playboy
Date: Feb 1985
Source URL:
http://www.playboy.com/magazine/playboy-interview-steve-jobs

83. Education computer affecting

Computers themselves, and software yet to be developed, will revolutionize the way we learn. We formed something called the Apple Education Foundation, and we give several million dollars in cash and equipment to people doing exploratory work with educational software and to schools that can't afford computers. We also wanted Macintosh to become the computer of choice in colleges, just as the Apple II is for grade and high schools. So we looked for six universities that were out to make large-scale commitments to personal computers—by large, meaning more than 1000 apiece—and instead of six, we found 24. We asked the colleges if they would invest at least $2,000,000 each to be part of the Macintosh program. All 24—including the entire Ivy League—did. So in less than a year, Macintosh has become the standard in college computing. I could ship every Macintosh we make this year just to those 24 colleges. We can't, of course, but the demand is there.

Name: Playboy Interview: Steven Jobs (David Sheff)
Published in: Playboy
Date: Feb 1985
Source URL:
http://www.playboy.com/magazine/playboy-interview-steve-jobs

84. Politics

No, none of those people care about the money. I mean, a lot of them made a lot of money, but they don't really care. Their lifestyles haven't particularly changed. It was the chance to actually try something, to fail, to succeed, to grow. Politics wasn't the place to be these past ten years if you were eager to try things out. As someone who hasn't turned 30 yet, I think your 20s are the time to be impatient, and a lot of these people's idealism would have been deeply frustrated in politics; it would have been blunted. I think it takes a crisis for something to occur in America. And I believe there's going to be a crisis of significant proportions in the early Nineties as these problems our political leaders should have been addressing boil up to the surface. And that's when a lot of these people are going to bring both their practical experience and their idealism into the political realm. You're going to see the best-trained generation ever to go into politics. They're going to know how to choose people, how to get things done, how to lead.

Name: Playboy Interview: Steven Jobs (David Sheff)
Published in: Playboy
Date: Feb 1985
Source URL:
http://www.playboy.com/magazine/playboy-interview-steve-jobs

85. Problem finding the funds

We're making the largest investment of capital that humankind has ever made in weapons over the next five years. We have decided, as a society, that that's where we should put our money, and that raises the deficits and, thus, the cost of our capital. Meanwhile, Japan, our nearest competitor on the next technological frontier—the semiconductor industry—has shaped its tax structure, its entire society, toward raising the capital to invest in that area. You get the feeling that connections aren't made in America between things like building weapons and the fact that we might lose our semiconductor industry. We have to educate ourselves to that danger.

Name: Playboy Interview: Steven Jobs (David Sheff)
Published in: Playboy
Date: Feb 1985
Source URL:
http://www.playboy.com/magazine/playboy-interview-steve-jobs

86. Computers will help

Well, I'll tell you a story. I saw a video tape that we weren't supposed to see. It was prepared for the Joint Chiefs of Staff. By watching the tape, we discovered that, at least as of a few years ago, every tactical nuclear weapon in Europe manned by U.S. personnel was targeted by an Apple II computer. Now, we didn't sell computers to the military; they went out and bought them at a dealer's, I guess. But it didn't make us feel good to know that our computers were being used to target nuclear weapons in Europe. The only bright side of it was that at least they weren't [Radio Shack] TRS-80s!
Thank God for that. The point is that tools are always going to be used for certain things we don't find personally pleasing. And it's ultimately the wisdom of people, not the tools themselves, that is going to determine whether or not these things are used in positive, productive ways.

Name: Playboy Interview: Steven Jobs (David Sheff)
Published in: Playboy
Date: Feb 1985
Source URL:
http://www.playboy.com/magazine/playboy-interview-steve-jobs

87. Computers and software near future

Thus far, we're pretty much using our computers as good servants. We ask them to do something, we ask them to do some operation like a spread sheet, we ask them to take our key strokes and make a letter out of them, and they do that pretty well. And you'll see more and more perfection of that—computer as servant. But the next thing is going to be computer as guide or agent. And what that means is that it's going to do more in terms of anticipating what we want and doing it for us, noticing connections and patterns in what we do, asking us if this is some sort of generic thing we'd like to do regularly, so that we're going to have, as an example, the concept of triggers. We're going to be able to ask our computers to monitor things for us, and when certain conditions happen, are triggered, the computers will take certain actions and inform us after the fact.

Name: Playboy Interview: Steven Jobs (David Sheff)
Published in: Playboy
Date: Feb 1985
Source URL:
http://www.playboy.com/magazine/playboy-interview-steve-jobs

88. Virtually overnight

I used to think about selling 1,000,000 computers a year, but it was just a thought. When it actually happens, it's a totally different thing. So it was, "Holy shit, it's actually coming true!" But what's hard to explain is that this does not feel like overnight. Next year will be my tenth year. I had never done anything longer than a year in my life. Six months, for me, was a long time when we started Apple. So this has been my life since I've been sort of a free-willed adult. Each year has been so robust with problems and successes and learning experiences and human experiences that a year is a lifetime at Apple. So this has been ten lifetimes.

Name: Playboy Interview: Steven Jobs (David Sheff)
Published in: Playboy
Date: Feb 1985
Source URL:
http://www.playboy.com/magazine/playboy-interview-steve-jobs

89. Want to do with the rest of this lifetime

There's an old Hindu saying that comes into my mind occasionally: "For the first 30 years of your life, you make your habits. For the last 30 years of your life, your habits make you." As I'm going to be 30 in February, the thought has crossed my mind.

Name: Playboy Interview: Steven Jobs (David Sheff)
Published in: Playboy
Date: Feb 1985
Source URL:
http://www.playboy.com/magazine/playboy-interview-steve-jobs

90. Money means

I still don't understand it. It's a large responsibility to have more than you can spend in your lifetime— and I feel I have to spend it. If you die, you certainly don't want to leave a large amount to your children. It will just ruin their lives. And if you die without kids, it will all go to the Government. Almost everyone would think that he could invest the money back into humanity in a much more astute way than the Government could. The challenges are to figure out how to live with it and to reinvest it back than the Government could. The challenges are to figure out how to live with it and to reinvest it back into the world, which means either giving it away or using it to express your concerns or values.

Name: Playboy Interview: Steven Jobs (David Sheff)
Published in: Playboy
Date: Feb 1985
Source URL:
http://www.playboy.com/magazine/playboy-interview-steve-jobs

91. Virtuous or extravagances

Well, my favorite things in life are books, sushi and.... My favorite things in life don't cost any money. It's really clear that the most precious resource we all have is time. As it is, I pay a price by not having much of a personal life. I don't have the time to pursue love affairs or to tour small towns in Italy and sit in cafes and eat tomato-and-mozzarella salad. Occasionally, I spend a little money to save myself a hassle, which means time. And that's the extent of it. I bought an apartment in New York, but it's because I love that city. I'm trying to educate myself, being from a small town in California, not having grown up with the sophistication and culture of a large city. I consider it part of my education. You know, there are many people at Apple who can buy everything that they could ever possibly want and still have most of their money unspent. I hate talking about this as a problem; people are going to read this and think, Yeah, well, give me your problem. They're going to think I'm an arrogant little asshole.

Name: Playboy Interview: Steven Jobs (David Sheff)
Published in: Playboy
Date: Feb 1985
Source URL:
http://www.playboy.com/magazine/playboy-interview-steve-jobs

92. My Job

We have an environment where excellence is really expected. What's really great is to be open when [the work] is not great. My best contribution is not settling for anything but really good stuff, in all the details. That's my job — to make sure everything is great.

Source: 1983, quoted in Steven Levy's Eulogy

93. IMac

When people look at an iMac, they think the design is really great, but most people don't understand it's not skin deep,' he said. 'There's a reason why, after two years, people haven't been able to copy the iMac. It's not just surface. The reason the iMac doesn't have a fan is engineering. It took a ton of engineering and that's true for the Cube and everything else.

Source: 2000, quoted in Steven Levy's Eulogy |

94. Feelings for Apple

Much of the industry has lived off the Macintosh for over ten years now, slowly copying the Mac's revolutionary user interface. Now the time has come for new innovation, and where better than Apple for this to spring from? Who else has consistently led this industry--first with the Apple II, then the Macintosh and Laser Writer? With this merger, the advanced software from NeXT will be married with Apple's very high-volume hardware platforms and marketing channels to create another breakthrough, leapfrogging existing platforms, and fueling Apple and the industry copy cats for the next ten years and beyond. I still have very deep feelings for Apple, and it gives me great joy to play a role in architecting Apple's future.

Source: Apple press release, Dec. 20 1996

95. About Microsoft

They are shamelessly trying to copy us. I think the most telling thing is that Tiger will ship at the end of the month and Longhorn is still two years out. They can't even copy fast.

Source: Apple shareholders meeting, Apr. 21 2005

96. Industry-leading products

When [people] see the iMac, for example, they think we really can produce industry-leading products like this. It's not about charisma and personality, it's about results and products and those very bedrock things that are why people at Apple and outside of Apple are getting more excited about the company and what Apple stands for and what its potential is to contribute to the industry.

Source: Business Week, May 12 1998

97. My Mantras

The organization is clean and simple to understand, and very accountable. Everything just got simpler. That's been one of my mantras -- focus and simplicity. Simple can be harder than complex: You have to work hard to get your thinking clean to make it simple. But it's worth it in the end because once you get there, you can move mountains.

Source: Business Week, May 12 1998

98. Apple's customers are loyal

I get asked a lot why Apple's customers are so loyal. It's not because they belong to the Church of Mac! That's ridiculous. It's because when you buy our products, and three months later you get stuck on something, you quickly figure out [how to get past it]. And you think, 'Wow, someone over there at Apple actually thought of this!' And then three months later you try to do something you hadn't tried before, and it works, and you think 'Hey, they thought of that, too.' And then six months later it happens again. There's almost no product in the world that you have that experience with, but you have it with a Mac.

Source: Business Week, Oct. 12 2004

99. Monopolies lost

And how are monopolies lost? Think about it. Some very good product people invent some very good products, and the company achieves a monopoly. But after that, the product people aren't the ones that drive the company forward anymore. It's the marketing guys or the ones who expand the business into Latin America or whatever. Because what's the point of focusing on making the product even better when the only company you can take business from is yourself? So a different group of people start to move up. And who usually ends up running the show? The sales guy. John Akers at IBM is the consummate example. Then one day, the monopoly expires for whatever reason. But by then the best product people have left, or they're no longer listened to. And so the company goes through this tumultuous time, and it either survives or it doesn't. Look at Microsoft — who's running Microsoft? (interviewer: Steve Ballmer.) Right, the sales guy. Case closed. And that's what happened at Apple, as well.

Source: Business Week, Oct. 12 2004

100. Busy

We're both busy and we both don't have a lot of time to learn how to use a washing machine or to use a phone - you get one of the phones now and you're never going to learn more than 5 per cent of the features. You're never going to use more than 5 per cent, and, uh, it's very complicated. So you end up using just 5 per cent. It's insane: we all have busy lives, we have jobs and we have interests and some of us have children, everyone's lives are just getting busier, not less busy, in this busy society. You just don't have time to learn this stuff, and every thing's getting more complicated.

Source: Business Week, Oct. 12 2004

101. Whole experiences

That was one of the things that came out most clearly from this whole experience [with cancer]. I realized that I love my life. I really do. I've got the greatest family in the world, and I've got my work. And that's pretty much all I do. I don't socialize much or go to conferences. I love my family, and I love running Apple, and I love Pixar. And I get to do that. I'm very lucky.

Source: Business Week, Oct. 12 2004

102. Reason

The reason I went back to Apple is that I feel like the world would be a better place with Apple in it than not. And it's hard to imagine the world without Apple now.

Source: Financial Times, Jan. 29 2010

103. Four things for users

We're still heavily into the box. We love the box. We have amazing computers today, and amazing hardware in the pipeline. I still spend a lot of my time working on new computers, and it will always be a primal thing for Apple. But the user experience is what we care about most, and we're expanding that experience beyond the box by making better use of the Internet. The user experience now entails four things: the hardware, the operating system, the applications, and the Net. We want to do all four uniquely well for our customers.

Source: Fortune, Jan. 24 2000

104. Starting

When I got started I was 20 or 21, and my role models were the semiconductor guys like Robert Noyce and Andy Grove of Intel, and of course Bill Hewlett and David Packard. They were out not so much to make money as to change the world and to build companies that could keep growing and changing. They left incredible legacies. [...] the rewarding thing isn't merely to start a company or to take it public. It's like when you're a parent. Although the birth experience is a miracle, what's truly rewarding is living with your child and helping him grow up.

Source: Fortune, Jan. 24 2000

105. People requirement

It's not about pop culture, and it's not about fooling people, and it's not about convincing people that they want something they don't. We figure out what we want. And I think we're pretty good at having the right discipline to think through whether a lot of other people are going to want it, too. That's what we get paid to do. So you can't go out and ask people, you know, what the next big [thing.] There's a great quote by Henry Ford, right? He said, 'If I'd have asked my customers what they wanted, they would have told me 'A faster horse.'

Source: Fortune, Mar. 7 2008

106. Focus

We tend to focus much more. People think focus means saying yes to the thing you've got to focus on. But that's not what it means at all. It means saying no to the hundred other good ideas that there are. You have to pick carefully. I'm actually as proud of many of the things we haven't done as the things we have done.

Source: Fortune, Mar. 7 2008

107. Recruiting

Recruiting is hard. It's just finding the needles in the haystack. We do it ourselves and we spend a lot of time at it. I've participated in the hiring of maybe 5,000-plus people in my life. So I take it very seriously. You can't know enough in a one-hour interview. So, in the end, it's ultimately based on your gut. How do I feel about this person? What are they like when they're challenged? Why are they here? I ask everybody that: 'Why are you here?' The answers themselves are not what you're looking for. It's the meta-data.

Source: Fortune, Mar. 7 2008

108. Capable people

We've got really capable people at Apple. I made Tim [Cook] COO and gave him the Mac division and he's done brilliantly. I mean, some people say, 'Oh, God, if [Jobs] got run over by a bus, Apple would be in trouble.' And, you know, I think it wouldn't be a party, but there are really capable people at Apple. And the board would have some good choices about who to pick as CEO. My job is to make the whole executive team good enough to be successors, so that's what I try to do.

Source: Fortune, Mar. 7 2008

109. Sort

We've got 25,000 people at Apple. About 10,000 of them are in the stores. And my job is to work with sort of the top 100 people, that's what I do. That doesn't mean they're all vice presidents. Some of them are just key individual contributors. So when a good idea comes, you know, part of my job is to move it around, just see what different people think, get people talking about it, argue with people about it, get ideas moving among that group of 100 people, get different people together to explore different aspects of it quietly, and, you know - just explore things.

Source: Fortune, Mar. 7 2008

110. Chosen

We don't get a chance to do that many things, and every one should be really excellent. Because this is our life. Life is brief, and then you die, you know? So this is what we've chosen to do with our life. We could be sitting in a monastery somewhere in Japan.

Source: Fortune, Mar. 7 2008

111. People off

when we laid some people off at Apple a year ago, or
when I have to take people out of their jobs, it's harder
for me now. Much harder. I do it because that's my job.
But when I look at people when this happens, I also
think of them as being 5 years old. And I think that
person could be me coming home to tell my wife and
kids that I just got laid off. Or that could be one of my
kids in 20 years. I never took it so personally before.
Life is short, and we're all going to die really soon. It's
true, you know.

Source: Fortune, Nov. 9 1998

112. TV and Computers

You go to your TV when you want to turn your brain
off. You go to your computer when you want to turn
your brain on. Those are not the same.

Source: Fortune, Nov. 9 1998

113. Building

The only purpose for me in building a company is so that it can make products. Of course, building a very strong company and a foundation of talent and culture is essential over the long run to keep making great products. On the other hand, to me, the company is one of humanity's most amazing inventions. It's totally abstract. Sure, you have to build something with bricks and mortar to put the people in, but basically a company is this abstract construct we've invented, and it's incredibly powerful.

Source: Fortune, Nov. 9 1998

114. My heroes

My heroes--Dave Packard, for example, left all his money to his foundation; Bob Noyce [the late co-founder of Intel] was another. I'm old enough to have been able to know these guys. I met Andy Grove when I was 21. I called him and told him I'd heard he was really good at operations and asked if I could take him out to lunch. I did that with others too. These guys were all company builders, and the gestalt of Silicon Valley at that time made a big impression on me. There are people around here who start companies just to make money, but the great companies, well, that's not what they're about.

Source: Fortune, Nov. 9 1998

115. About life

I don't think much about my time of life. I just get up in the morning and it's a new day. Somebody told me when I was 17 to live each day as if it were my last, and that one day I'd be right. I am at a stage where I don't have to do things just to get by. But then I've always been that way because I've never really cared about money that much. I guess what I'm trying to say is that I feel the same way now as I felt when I was 17.

Source: Fortune, Nov. 9 1998

116. Stay hungry. Stay foolish

That's the moment that an artist really decides who he or she is. If they keep on risking failure, they're still artists. Dylan and Picasso were always risking failure. This Apple thing is that way for me. I don't want to fail, of course. But even though I didn't know how bad things really were, I still had a lot to think about before I said yes. I had to consider the implications for Pixar, for my family, for my reputation. I decided that I didn't really care, because this is what I want to do. If I try my best and fail, well, I tried my best. What makes you become conservative is realising that you have something to lose. Remember THE WHOLE EARTH CATALOG? The last edition had a photo on the back cover of a remote country road you might find yourself on while hitch-hiking up to Oregon. It was a beautiful shot, and it had a caption that really grabbed me. It said: 'Stay hungry. Stay foolish.' It wasn't an ad for anything--just one of Stewart Brand's profound statements. It's wisdom. 'Stay hungry. Stay foolish.'

Source: Fortune, Nov. 9 1998

117. Regret

But I think the things you most regret in life are things you didn't do. What you really regret was never asking that girl to dance. In business, if I knew earlier what I know now, I'd have probably done some things a lot better than I did, but I also would've probably done some other things a lot worse. But so what? It's more important to be engaged in the present.

Source: Fortune, Nov. 9 1998

118. Aesthetic judgement

You're asking, where does aesthetic judgement come from? With many things—high-performance auto mobiles, for example—the aesthetic comes right from the function, and I suppose electronics is no different. But I've also found that the best companies pay attention to aesthetics. They take the extra time to lay out grids and proportion things appropriately, and it seems to pay off for them. I mean, beyond the functional benefits, the aesthetic communicates something about how they think of themselves, their sense of discipline in engineering, how they run their company, stuff like that.

Source: Inc, Apr. 1989

119. About his employees

If they are working in an environment where excellence is expected, then they will do excellent work without anything but self-motivation. I'm talking about an environment in which excellence is noticed and respected and is in the culture. If you have that, you don't have to tell people to do excellent work. They understand it from their surroundings.

Source: Inc, Apr. 1989

120. Culture at NeXT

The culture at NeXT definitely rewards independent thought, and we often have constructive disagreements—at all levels. It doesn't take a new person long to see that people feel fine about openly disagreeing with me. That doesn't mean I can't disagree with them, but it does mean that the best ideas win. Our attitude is that we want the best. Don't get hung up on who owns the idea. Pick the best one, and let's go.

Source: Inc, Apr. 1989

121. Manufacturing

I think the same philosophy that drives the product has to drive everything else if you want to have a great company. Manufacturing, for example, [...] demands just as much thought and strategy as the product. If you don't pay attention to your manufacturing, it will limit the kind of product you can build and engineer. Some companies view manufacturing as a necessary evil, and some view it as something more neutral. But we view it instead as a tremendous opportunity to gain a competitive advantage. [I've thought that] ever since I visited Japan in the early '80s. And let me add that the same is true of sales and marketing. You need a sales and marketing organisation that is oriented toward educating customers rather than just taking orders, providing a real service rather than moving boxes. This is extremely important.

Source: Inc, Apr. 1989

122. Silicon Valley

Well, I don't know what this Valley is. I work at Apple. I'm there so many hours a day and I don't visit other places; I'm not an expert on Silicon Valley. What I do see is a small group of people who are artists and care more about their art than they do about almost anything else. It's more important than finding a girlfriend, it's more important... than cooking a meal, it's more important than joining the Marines, it's more important than whatever. Look at the way artists work. They're not typically the most 'balanced' people in the world. Now, yes, we have a few workaholics here who are trying to escape other things, of course. But the majority of people out here have made very conscious decisions; they really have.

Source: Newsweek, fall 1984

123. Role models

Even though some people have come out with neat products, if their company is perceived as a sweatshop or a revolving door, it's not considered much of a success. Remember, the role models were Hewlett and Packard. Their main achievement was that they built a company. Nobody remembers their first frequency-counter, their first audio oscillator, their first this or that. And they sell so many products now that no one person really symbolises the company. [...] And they built a company and they lived that philosophy for 35 or 40 years and that's why they're heroes. Hewlett and Packard started what became the Valley.

Source: Newsweek, fall 1984

124. Music mattered

I was very lucky to grow up in a time when music really mattered. It wasn't just something in the background; it really mattered to a generation of kids growing up. It really changed the world. I think that music faded in importance for a while, and the iPod has helped to bring music back into people's lives in a really meaningful way. Music is so deep within all of us, but it's easy to go for a day or a week or a month or a year without really listening to music. And the iPod has changed that for tens of millions of people, and that makes me really happy, because I think music is good for the soul.

Source: Newsweek, Oct. 16 2006

125. Genes

So if Apple just becomes a place where computers are a commodity item and where the romance is gone, and where people forget that computers are the most incredible invention that man has ever invented, then I'll feel I have lost Apple. But if I'm a million miles away and all those people still feel those things and they're still working to make the next great personal computer, then I will feel that my genes are still in there.

126. Yardstick

And so I haven't got any sort of odd chip on my shoulder about proving anything to myself or anybody else. And remember, though the outside world looks at success from a numerical point of view, my yardstick might be quite different than that. My yardstick may be how every computer that's designed from here on out will have to be at least as good as a Macintosh.

Source: Newsweek, Sep. 29 1985

127. My philosophy

You know, my philosophy is—it's always been very simple. And it has its flaws, which I'll go into. My philosophy is that everything starts with a great product. So, you know, I obviously believed in listening to customers, but customers can't tell you about the next breakthrough that's going to happen next year that's going to change the whole industry. So you have to listen very carefully. But then you have to go and sort of stow away—you have to go hide away with people that really understand the technology, but also really care about the customers, and dream up this next breakthrough. And that's my perspective, that everything starts with a great product. And that has its flaws. I have certainly been accused of not listening to the customers enough. And I think there is probably a certain amount of that that's valid.

Source: Newsweek, Sep. 29 1985

128. Influencing the future

At Apple, people are putting in 18-hour days. We attract a different type of person—a person who doesn't want to wait five or ten years to have someone take a giant risk on him or her. Someone who really wants to get in a little over his head and make a little dent in the universe. We are aware that we are doing something significant. We're here at the beginning of it and we're able to shape how it goes. Everyone here has the sense that right now is one of those moments when we are influencing the future.

Source: Playboy, Feb. 1985

129. Mac & PCjr

How come the Mac group produced Mac and the people at IBM produced the PCjr? We think the Mac will sell zillions, but we didn't build Mac for anybody else. We built it for ourselves. We were the group of people who were going to judge whether it was great or not. We weren't going to go out and do market research. We just wanted to build the best thing we could build. When you're a carpenter making a beautiful chest of drawers, you're not going to use a piece of plywood on the back, even though it faces the wall and nobody will ever see it. You'll know it's there, so you're going to use a beautiful piece of wood on the back. For you to sleep well at night, the aesthetic, the quality, has to be carried all the way through. PLAYBOY: Are you saying that the people who made the PCjr don't have that kind of pride in the product? JOBS: If they did, they wouldn't have turned out the PCjr.

Source: Playboy, Feb. 1985

130. Machinist

My father was a machinist, and he was a sort of genius with his hands. He can fix anything and make it work and take any mechanical thing apart and get it back together. That was my first glimpse of it. I started to gravitate more toward electronics, and he used to get me things I could take apart and put back together.

Source: Playboy, Feb. 1985

131. Woz & I

Woz and I are different in most ways, but there are some ways in which we're the same, and we're very close in those ways. We're sort of like two planets in their own orbits that every so often intersect. It wasn't just computers, either. Woz and I very much liked Bob Dylan's poetry, and we spent a lot of time thinking about a lot of that stuff. This was California. You could get LSD fresh made from Stanford. You could sleep on the beach at night with your girlfriend. California has a sense of experimentation and a sense of openness— openness to new possibilities. Besides Dylan, I was interested in Eastern mysticism, which hit the shores at about the same time. When I went to college at Reed, in Oregon, there was a constant flow of people stopping by, from Timothy Leary and Richard Alpert to Gary Snyder. There was a constant flow of intellectual questioning about the truth of life. That was a time when every college student in this country read BE HERE NOW and DIET FOR A SMALL PLANET.

Source: Playboy, Feb. 1985

132. Biological parents

I think it's quite a natural curiosity for adopted people to want to understand where certain traits come from. But I'm mostly an environmentalist. I think the way you are raised and your values and most of your world view come from the experiences you had as you grew up. But some things aren't accounted for that way. I think it's quite natural to have a curiosity about it.

Source: Playboy, Feb. 1985

133. Dr. Edwin Land

Dr. Edwin Land was a troublemaker. He dropped out of Harvard and founded Polaroid. Not only was he one of the great inventors of our time but, more important, he saw the intersection of art and science and business and built an organisation to reflect that. Polaroid did that for some years, but eventually Dr. Land, one of those brilliant troublemakers, was asked to leave his own company—which is one of the dumbest things I've ever heard of. [...] The man is a national treasure. I don't understand why people like that can't be held up as models: This is the most incredible thing to be—not an astronaut, not a football player—but this.

Source: Playboy, Feb. 1985

134. Makes feel old

It makes me feel old, sometimes, when I speak at a campus and I find that what students are most in awe of is the fact that I'm a millionaire. When I went to school, it was right after the Sixties and before this general wave of practical purposefulness had set in. Now students aren't even thinking in idealistic terms, or at least nowhere near as much. They certainly are not letting any of the philosophical issues of the day take up too much of their time as they study their business majors. The idealistic wind of the Sixties was still at our backs, though, and most of the people I know who are my age have that ingrained in them forever.

Source: Playboy, Feb. 1985

135. Computers as Servants

Thus far, we're pretty much using our computers as good servants. We ask them to do something, we ask them to do some operation like a spread sheet, we ask them to take our key strokes and make a letter out of them, and they do that pretty well. And you'll see more and more perfection of that—computer as servant. But the next thing is going to be computer as guide or agent. And what that means is that it's going to do more in terms of anticipating what we want and doing it for us, noticing connections and patterns in what we do, asking us if this is some sort of generic thing we'd like to do regularly, so that we're going to have, as an example, the concept of triggers. We're going to be able to ask our computers to monitor things for us, and when certain conditions happen, are triggered, the computers will take certain actions and inform us after the fact.

Source: Playboy, Feb. 1985

136. Tapestry

I'll always stay connected with Apple. I hope that throughout my life I'll sort of have the thread of my life and the thread of Apple weave in and out of each other, like a tapestry. There may be a few years when I'm not there, but I'll always come back. And that's what I may try to do. The key thing to remember about me is that I'm still a student. I'm still in boot camp. If anyone is reading any of my thoughts, I'd keep that in mind. Don't take it all too seriously. If you want to live your life in a creative way, as an artist, you have to not look back too much. You have to be willing to take whatever you've done and whoever you were and throw them away.

Source: Playboy, Feb. 1985

137. Tools

A computer frees people from much of the menial work. Besides that, you are giving them a tool that encourages them to be creative. Remember, computers are tools. Tools help us do our work better.

Source: Playboy, Feb. 1985

138. Corrosive piece

The most corrosive piece of technology that I've ever seen is called television — but then, again, television, at its best, is magnificent.

Source: Rolling Stone, Dec. 25 2003

139. Microsoft goals

First I should tell you my theory about Microsoft. Microsoft has had two goals in the last 10 years. One was to copy the Mac, and the other was to copy Lotus' success in the spreadsheet — basically, the applications business. And over the course of the last 10 years, Microsoft accomplished both of those goals. And now they are completely lost. They were able to copy the Mac because the Mac was frozen in time. The Mac didn't change much for the last 10 years. It changed maybe 10 percent. It was a sitting duck. It's amazing that it took Microsoft 10 years to copy something that was a sitting duck.

Source: Rolling Stone, Jun. 16 1994

140. Fastest-moving industry

People say sometimes, 'You work in the fastest-moving industry in the world.' I don't feel that way. I think I work in one of the slowest. It seems to take forever to get anything done. All of the graphical-user interface stuff that we did with the Macintosh was pioneered at Xerox PARC [the company's legendary Palo Alto Research Center] and with Doug Engelbart at SRI [a future-oriented think tank at Stanford] in the mid-'70s. And here we are, just about the mid-'90s, and it's kind of commonplace now. But it's about a 10-to-20-year lag. That's a long time.

Source: Rolling Stone, Jun. 16 1994

141. Macintosh

The Macintosh was sort of like this wonderful romance in your life that you once had — and that produced about 10 million children. In a way it will never be over in your life. You'll still smell that romance every morning when you get up. And when you open the window, the cool air will hit your face, and you'll smell that romance in the air. And you'll see your children around, and you feel good about it. And nothing will ever make you feel bad about it.

Source: Rolling Stone, Jun. 16 1994

142. Optimistic

Technology is nothing. What's important is that you have a faith in people, that they're basically good and smart, and if you give them tools, they'll do wonderful things with them. It's not the tools that you have faith in — tools are just tools. They work, or they don't work. It's people you have faith in or not. Yeah, sure, I'm still optimistic I mean, I get pessimistic sometimes but not for long.

Source: Rolling Stone, Jun. 16 1994

143. Internet

The Internet is nothing new. It has been happening for 10 years. Finally, now, the wave is cresting on the general computer user. And I love it. I think the den is far more interesting than the living room. Putting the Internet into people's houses is going to be really what the information superhighway is all about, not digital convergence in the set-top box. All that's going to do is put the video rental stores out of business and save me a trip to rent my movie. I'm not very excited about that. I'm not excited about home shopping. I'm very excited about having the Internet in my den.

Source: Rolling Stone, Jun. 16 1994

144. Science and Aesthetics

To make Apple a great $10 billion company. Apple has the opportunity to set a new example of how great an American corporation can be, sort of an intersection between science and aesthetics. Something happens to companies when they get to be a few million dollars – their souls go away. And that's the biggest thing I'll be measured on: Were we able to grow a $10 billion company that didn't lose its soul?

Source: Rolling Stone, Mar. 1984

145. No idea

I naively chose a college that was almost as expensive as Stanford, and all of my working-class parents' savings were being spent on my college tuition. After six months, I couldn't see the value in it. I had no idea what I wanted to do with my life and no idea how college was going to help me figure it out. And here I was spending all of the money my parents had saved their entire life. So I decided to drop out and trust that it would all work out OK. It was pretty scary at the time, but looking back it was one of the best decisions I ever made. The minute I dropped out I could stop taking the required classes that didn't interest me, and begin dropping in on the ones that looked interesting.

Source: Stanford commencement addres, Jun. 12 2005

146. Dropped out

Because I had dropped out and didn't have to take the normal classes, I decided to take a calligraphy class to learn how to do this [...] and I found it fascinating. None of this had even a hope of any practical application in my life. But ten years later, when we were designing the first Macintosh computer, it all came back to me. And we designed it all into the Mac. It was the first computer with beautiful typography. If I had never dropped in on that single course in college, the Mac would have never had multiple typefaces or proportionally spaced fonts. And since Windows just copied the Mac, it's likely that no personal computer would have them.

Source: Stanford commencement addres, Jun. 12 2005

147. Don't settle

Sometimes life hits you in the head with a brick. Don't lose faith. I'm convinced that the only thing that kept me going was that I loved what I did. You've got to find what you love. And that is as true for your work as it is for your lovers. Your work is going to fill a large part of your life, and the only way to be truly satisfied is to do what you believe is great work. And the only way to do great work is to love what you do. If you haven't found it yet, keep looking. Don't settle. As with all matters of the heart, you'll know when you find it. And, like any great relationship, it just gets better and better as the years roll on. So keep looking until you find it. Don't settle.

Source: Stanford commencement addres, Jun. 12 2005

148. Die

No one wants to die. Even people who want to go to heaven don't want to die to get there. And yet death is the destination we all share. No one has ever escaped it. And that is as it should be, because Death is very likely the single best invention of Life. It is Life's change agent. It clears out the old to make way for the new. Right now the new is you, but someday not too long from now, you will gradually become the old and be cleared away. Sorry to be so dramatic, but it is quite true. Your time is limited, so don't waste it living someone else's life. Don't be trapped by dogma — which is living with the results of other people's thinking. Don't let the noise of others' opinions drown out your own inner voice. And most important, have the courage to follow your heart and intuition. They somehow already know what you truly want to become. Everything else is secondary.

Source: Stanford commencement addres, Jun. 12 2005

149. Contribution

My best contribution to the group is not settling for anything but really good stuff. A lot of times, people don't do great things because great things really aren't expected of them, and nobody ever really demands that they try, and nobody says, 'Hey, that's the culture here'. If you set that up, people will do things that are greater than they ever thought they could be. Really some great work that will go down in history.

Source: Steve Jobs in 1984, quoted in The Perfect Thing by Steven Levy

150. Boredom

I'm a big believer in boredom. Boredom allows one to indulge in curiosity and out of curiosity comes everything. All the [technology] stuff is wonderful, but having nothing to do can be wonderful, too.

Source: Steven Levy's Eulogy |

151. Detractors

Some detractors like those at Listen.com say that downloading isn't the most popular feature on their music service Rhapsody. What's your response? Well, that's correct. Downloading sucks on their service. You download a track and you can't burn it to a CD without paying them more money—you can't put it on your MP3 player, you can't put it on multiple computers—it sucks! So of course nobody downloads! You pay extra to download even on top of subscription fees. No wonder they have hardly any download traffic—[they] hardly even have any subscribers.

Source: Technologizer, Apr. 28 2003

152. Energy

The amount of time you spend shopping and preparing and eating food is enormous. The amount of energy your body spends digesting the food in many cases exceeds the energy we get from the food.

Source: Time Magazine, Jan. 3 1983

153. Compete

I would rather compete with Sony than compete in another product category with Microsoft. That's because Sony has to rely on other companies to make its software. We're the only company that owns the whole widget--the hardware, the software and the operating system. We can take full responsibility for the user experience. We can do things that the other guy can't do.

Source: Time Magazine, Jan. 14 2002

154. iMac launch

The people around here--some of them left. Actually, some of them I got rid of. But most of them said, 'Oh, my God, now I get it.' We've been doing this now for seven years, and everybody here gets it. And if they don't, they're gone.

Source: Time Magazine, Oct. 16 2005

155. Apple Cafeteria

This is the nicest corporate cafe I've ever seen. When we got here this was dog food. There was this company called Guggeinheim that it was farmed out to and it was just shit. And finally we fired them and got this friend of mine who runs Il Fourniao restaurant to come and he did everything and now it's great.

Source: Time Magazine, Oct. 18 2000

156. Bill Gates

I've read something that Bill Gates said about six
months ago. He said, 'I worked really, really hard in my
20s.' And I know what he means, because I worked
really, really hard in my 20s too. Literally, you know, 7
days a week, a lot of hours every day. And it actually is
a wonderful thing to do, because you can get a lot
done. But you can't do it forever, and you don't want
to do it forever, and you have to come up with ways of
figuring out what the most important things are and
working with other people even more.

Source: Time Magazine, Oct. 18 2000

157. Different things

There's different things in life you can do. You can
become a painter, you can become a sculptor. You can
make something by yourself. But that's not what I do. I
do the other thing, which is, you work at things that
one person can't do, and that you need large numbers
of people to do. I know people like symbols, but it's
always unsettling when people write stories about me,
because they tend to overlook a lot of other people.

Source: Time Magazine, Oct. 18 2000 |

158. Interact

The number of people I get to interact with in this company is probably about 50 on a regular basis. Maybe 100. And one of the things that I've always felt is that most things in life, if you get something twice as good as average you're doing phenomenally well. Usually the best is about 30% better than average. Two to one's a big delta. But hat became really clear to me in my work life was that, for instance, [Steve] Woz[niak] was 25 to 50 times better than average. And I found that there were these incredibly great people at doing certain things, and you couldn't replace one of these people with 50 average people. They could just do stuff that no number of average people could do. [...]. And so I have spent my work life trying to find and recruit and retain and work with these kind of people. My #1 job here at Apple is to make sure that the top 100 people are A+ players. And everything else will take care of itself.

Source: Time Magazine, Oct. 18 2000

159. Problem with Microsoft

The only problem with Microsoft is they just have no taste. They have absolutely no taste. And I don't mean that in a small way, I mean that in a big way, in the sense that they don't think of original ideas, and they don't bring much culture into their products. I am saddened, not by Microsoft's success — I have no problem with their success. They've earned their success, for the most part. I have a problem with the fact that they just make really third-rate products.

Source: Triumph of the Nerds, 1995

160. Brutal

I'm brutally honest, because the price of admission to being in the room with me is I get to tell you your full of shit if you're full of shit, and you get to say to me I'm full of shit, and we have some rip-roaring fights. And that keeps the B players, the bozos, from larding the organisation, only the A players survive. And the people who do survive, say, 'Yeah, he was rough.' They say things even worse than 'He cut in line in front of me,' but they say, 'This was the greatest ride I've ever had, and I would not give it up for anything.'

Source: Walter Isaacson interview, Fortune, Dec. 27 2011

161. Observation

My observation, is that the doers are the major thinkers. The people that really create the things that change this industry are both the thinker and doer in one person. And if we really go back and we examine, you know, did Leonardo have a guy off to the side that was thinking five years out in the future what he would paint or the technology he would use to paint it, of course not. Leonardo was the artist but he also mixed all his own paints. He also was a fairly good chemist. He knew about pigments, knew about human anatomy. And combining all of those skills together, the art and the science, the thinking and the doing, was what resulted in the exceptional result. And there is no difference in our industry. The people that have really made the contributions have been the thinkers and the doers. And a lot of people of course - it's very easy to take credit for the thinking. The doing is more concrete. But somebody, it's very easy to say 'oh I thought of this three years ago'. But usually when you dig a little deeper, you find that the people that really did it were also the people that really worked through the hard intellectual problems as well.

Source: WGBH, May 14 1990

162. Inherent abilities

I remember reading an article when I was about twelve years old. I think it might have been Scientific American, where they measured the efficiency of locomotion for all these species on planet earth. How many kilo calories did they expend to get from point A to point B? And the condor won, came in at the top of the list, surpassed everything else. And humans came in about a third of the way down the list, which was not such a great showing for the crown of creation. But somebody there had the imagination to test the efficiency of a human riding a bicycle. A human riding a bicycle blew away the condor all the way off the top of the list. And it made a really big impression on me that we humans are tool builders. And that we can fashion tools that amplify these inherent abilities that we have to spectacular magnitudes. And so for me, a computer has always been a bicycle of the mind. Something that takes us far beyond our inherent abilities. And I think we're just at the early stages of this tool.

Source: WGBH, May 14 1990

163. Comparing

There is a lot to be said for comparing [going from mainframes to the PC] to going from trains, from passenger trains to auto mobiles. And the advent of the auto mobiles gave us a personal freedom of transportation. In the same way the advent of the computer gave us the ability to start to use computers without having to convince other people that we needed to use computers. And the biggest effect of the personal computer revolution has been to allow millions and millions of people to experience computers themselves decades before they ever would have in the old paradigm. And to allow them to participate in the making of choices and controlling their own destiny using these tools.

Source: WGBH, May 14 1990

164. Speech

Right now, if you buy a computer system and you want to solve one of your problems, we immediately throw a big problem right in the middle of you and your problem which is learning how to use the computer. A substantial problem to overcome. Once you overcome that, it's a phenomenal tool. But there is a barrier of having to overcome that problem.

What we're trying to do ... is to remove that barrier so that someone can buy a computer system who knows nothing about it and directly attack their problem without learning how to program their computer.

Our whole company, our whole philosophical base, is founded on one principle. That principle is that there is something very special and very historically different that takes place when you have one computer and one person. Very different than if you have ten people and one computer.

Source: Speech in 1980

165. Much better

I don't think it's good that Apple's perceived as different. I think it's important that Apple's perceived as *much better*. If being different is essential to doing that, then we have to do that, but if we can be much better without being different, that'd be fine with me. I want to be much better.

166. Jobs' neighbourhood

We were in Jobs' neighbourhood two weekends ago having dinner with some friends of my parents, and we decided to take a walk in order to look at Steve Jobs' and Steve Young's houses, which are right next to each other. We headed over, and all of a sudden were alongside Jobs house. It's a really unusual and interesting house, but very understated and relatively small. You can just freely walk on the side walk right next to it. Well, we were walking along, and I heard dishes clattering, coming from his house, and I look over and there he was in his kitchen window, black turtle neck and all, washing dishes. He just looked up at us, maybe 15 feet away. Nothing in between us but a window, no tall fence (a short, decorative, waist-high one). And we just walked on and proceeded to admire the apple orchard he has in his front yard, and even walked up his driveway a little to see his tulip garden.

His neighbour, who we were walking with, told us that his security lives in the house next door, and he is under constant surveillance, but I still couldn't help but be shocked at how simple and unassuming his house was, and the fact that we saw him washing his dishes.

Source: Gawker, Mar 31, 2010

167. Hand Shake

I used to work at one of the Apple Stores here in New York. He was scheduled to come in, we didn't know exactly when. He got out of a town car out front, walked in, and right up to me - shaking my hand and saying, "Hi, I'm Steve Jobs! Is [name of the store manager] here?" When I said he was and called him, [Jobs] said he was going to run to the bathroom first - and went to the customer's bathroom (which anyone can use – and isn't exactly the cleanest). He came out, walked right back up to me, and started talking about the store. After about 5 min customers around us starting walking up asking to take pictures, and asking questions, when he promptly asked to be excused and left - back to the car and away.

We had all heard stories about his desire to not shake hands (he offered first), his desire to not be in public (he spent his entire time in full view in open areas of the store) and his general shitty attitude (he was super nice and cordial).

Source: Allen Paltrow, Oct 6, 2011

168. Spare parts

In 1998, Jobs decided that Airborne Logistics Services, a division of Airborne Express that maintained a parts warehouse for Apple in Grove City, Ohio, wasn't delivering spare parts quickly enough. According to Jeff Cooke, who ran Apple's customer-service department at the time, Jobs ordered him to find a replacement for ALS. When Cooke resisted, citing concerns that ALS would sue for breach of contract, he says Jobs told him that "there won't be any lawsuit. Just tell them if they f--- with us, they'll never get another f---ing dime from this company, ever," Cooke recalls. Jobs says he does not remember making the comment, but confirms that he was determined to drop ALS. Sure enough, Apple became embroiled in a lawsuit with ALS, which was settled in mid- 1999. Cooke resigned after just 100 days at Apple. "My stock options would be worth $10 million had I stayed, but I knew I couldn't have stood it--and he'd have fired me anyway," says Cooke. If some of Job's methods are distasteful, they do get results. After dumping ALS, Apple gave its spare-parts business to PC ServiceSource and demanded it slash the inventory by 75% in a matter of weeks, says former PC ServiceSource CEO Mark Hilz, now head of a Dallas real estate management company. "They got very, very, very results-oriented once Jobs got back there," says Hilz. "Under Steve Jobs, there's zero tolerance for not performing."

Source: Fortune, Jul 31, 2000

169. New iMacs

It's Monday morning, and Jobs is on stage at the Flint Center in Cupertino, obsessing. Tomorrow the auditorium will overflow with thousands of Apple loyalists; right now he's rehearsing the killer moment where he says, "Say hello to the new iMacs," and the machines glide out from behind the dark curtain and across the stage. But the current lighting leaves their translucence insufficiently vivid on the gigantic on stage screen. So Jobs wants the lights brighter and turned on earlier in the roll-out. The producer, Steph Adams, speaks into his headset, telling the backstage guys to yeah, just try it again, with the edgy tone of a man whose job consists of placating a perfectionist. No good. Jobs jogs halfway up the aisle and slouches into a center seat, his legs slung over the seat backs of the next row. "Let's keep doing it till we get it right, O.K.?" They go again. The iMacs are still under lighted. "No, no," Jobs whines, agonised. "This isn't working at all."

And again. Now the lights are bright enough, but they're still coming on too late. "I'm getting tired of asking about this," Jobs growls.

Again. And finally they get it right, the five impeccably lighted iMacs gleaming as they glide forward smoothly on the giant screen. "Oh! Right there! That's great!" Jobs yells, elated at the very notion of a universe capable of producing these insanely beautiful machines. "That's perfect!" he bellows, his voice booming across the empty auditorium. "Wooh!"

And you know what? He's right. The iMacs do look better when the lights come on earlier.

Source: Time Magazine, Oct 18, 1999

170. Do Not Engage

He walked past me and held the IL1 lobby door open. Steve Jobs. Holding the door for me. What?

That moment changed my life, and other former and current employees surely have moments like it. Whatever Steve was upset about that day was almost certainly more serious than anything I have faced in my career. Yet he still had the good sense to give me a smile and an act of courtesy. It taught me to never lose perspective and never forget who you're dealing with, no matter what else is going on.

Source: Matt Drance, Oct 7, 2011

171. Intern

I was an intern [at Apple in the summer of 2001] and one day the head of the intern program gathered the almost 100 interns into the Town Hall auditorium in Infinite Loop 4 for a "surprise guest speaker" that wasn't really much of a surprise: Steve Jobs. The meeting had no agenda but I had a hunch that when Steve (everyone who has ever worked at Apple just calls him "Steve") ended his remarks there would be a Q&A session. My mind started racing. This was probably going to be the one time in my life when I would have the chance to ask Steve Jobs a question and get a reply. This has *got* to be a good question. This was like getting a chance to shoot a basket with Michael Jordan, you want to take a good shot.

Source: Jonhatan Berger, Aug 25, 2011

172. Closest thing

The closest thing [Steve Jobs and I] ever had to an argument was when I left in 1985 to start a company to build a universal remote control. I went to [design agency of which Apple was a client] Frog Design to do the design. Steve dropped in there one day and he saw what they were designing for me and he threw it against the wall and said they could not do any work for me. "Anything you do for Woz, belongs to me." I was on my own, but I was still friendly with Apple. But Steve had a burst-out there. The people at Frog told me about it. That was the only time there was ever a fight between us, but it wasn't actually between us. Nobody has ever seen us having an argument.

Source: Steve Wozniak, interview with Dan Lyons, Oct 11, 2011

173. Diane Keaton

Diane Keaton, 65, says she met Jobs in the late '70s, when the late computer genius was her NYC neighbour. Steve wanted to meet the "Annie Hall" star, so she went over fora visit. But things went downhill fast.

"[A]ll he's talking about is the computer thing," Keaton recalls. "How the computer was going to take over the world. And I'm sitting there like, 'OK, right.' And he keeps talking about how everyone is going to have a computer in their life, in their world, in their home. And I'm going, 'Right, Right.'"

Unfortunately, all the tech talk didn't go over well with the actress, who says she never saw Jobs again. "[B]ecause obviously I just wasn't prepared for that. I thought, 'Is he nuts?'" But Keaton does regret leaving Steve: "Can you imagine? What an idiot I was."

Source: CNN The Marquee Blog, Dec 15, 2011

174. Argue

We're in a meeting at NeXT, before Steve went back to Apple. I've got my chief scientist. After the meeting, we leave and try to unravel the argument to figure out where Steve was wrong—because he was obviously wrong. And we couldn't do it. We're standing in the parking lot.

He sees us from his office, and he comes back out to argue with us some more. It was over a technical issue involving Objective C, a computer language. Why he would care about this was beyond me. I've never seen that kind of passion.

Source: Eric Schmidt, Business Week, Oct 6, 2011

175. iTunes

He thought that with iTunes, he could make it easier for people who wanted to respect intellectual copyright. So we had the idea to offer "Vertigo" for an iPod commercial, and we went out to see Steve at his house in Palo Alto and he was like, "What? You guys want to give me a song for a commercial? Wow, that's great, that's amazing." Then we said we wanted to be in the commercial, and he said "Maybe, yeah, I don't see why not."

Then we said we don't want to be paid, but we'd like a U2 iPod, a black one. His first response was, "That doesn't work at all. iPods are white!" But it turned out lots of people wanted them – and not because of U2. Because they were red and black!

Source: Bono, Rolling Stone, Oct 7, 2011

176. Clear thinker

He was a clear thinker, on lots of subjects, and I could turn to him. My actual last conversation with him was he called me because he was worried about my health, which is a clue to him. This tough guy was very tender, and he said, "I don't like the look of you, you look worn out," and I said, "What? I'm fine!" He wouldn't listen to me.

When I hurt my spine and I was in trouble, this package arrived of books and CDs and music and honey from their garden – tons of stuff arrived at the house. And so, yes, he was a captain of industry, a warrior for his companies. But I found him to be a very thoughtful friend, and a wonderfully detailed and interested parent of his kids, and lover of his wife.

Source: Bono, Rolling Stone, Oct 7, 2011

177. Business Insider

What is the significance of the employee numbers, since you were saying that you took seven because you wanted it. Michael Scott (Apple's first CEO): We had to have a payroll, and in order to minimise how much work we had to do, I had to sign up with Bank of America's payroll system, and those days you didn't have a choice. You had to assign employee numbers.

That was a dispute you get into — who gets number 1? One of the first things was that of course, each Steve wanted number 1. I know I didn't give it to Jobs because I thought that would be too much. I don't remember if it was Woz or Markkula that got number 1, but it didn't go to Jobs because I had enough problems anyway.

Source: Interview of Michael Scott, Business Insider, May 24, 2011

178. Challenge

Steve or me, and I think I won.

The other argument at the meetings was would Steve take his dirty feet and sandals off the table, because he sat at one end of the conference table, and Markkula sat at the other end chain smoking. So we had to have special filters in the attic in the ceiling to keep the room filter. I had the smokers on one side and the people with dirty feet on the other.

[Laughter from interviewer.]

It was not funny then. Everybody has their pet peeves.

Source: Interview of Michael Scott, Business Insider, May 24, 2011

179. Fight over

If we were negotiating price for parts,

we could negotiate a price with a vendor and at the last minute, Steve would come in and bang on the table and demand to get one more penny off. And of course they would give him one more penny off. Then he'd crow "well I see you didn't do as good a job as you could've getting the price down."

And I'm saying, "Yeah but that one more penny might've cost us a bit more ill will for times when parts are in short supply."

Source: Interview of Michael Scott, Business Insider, May 24, 2011

180. Garbage

Jobs imagines his garbage regularly not being emptied in his office, and when he asks the janitor why, he gets an excuse: The locks have been changed, and the janitor doesn't have a key. This is an acceptable excuse coming from someone who empties trash bins for a living. The janitor gets to explain why something went wrong. Senior people do not. "When you're the janitor," Jobs has repeatedly told incoming Vps, "reasons matter." He continues: "Somewhere between the janitor and the CEO, reasons stop mattering." That "Rubicon," he has said, "is crossed when you become a VP."

Source: Fortune, Aug 25, 2011

181. Courtyard at Apple

I saw Jobs was by chance in the courtyard at Apple headquarters 3½ years ago. I was there with my older son, then 15, to have lunch with an Apple friend. My son is a big Apple fan and user. By chance, we saw Jobs was walking along by himself, pecking away at his iPhone. I said hello, as did he -- and he then took my son aside to chat for several minutes, about technology and thinking large. My son was rapt.

It was a gracious thing for Jobs to do, with no pay off for himself. (I don't merit efforts to co-opt.) He later e-mailed me about the joys of parenthood. While Jobs was tone-deaf at times, he wasn't a jerk.

Source: David A. Kaplan, Fortune, Oct 11, 2011

182. Tough

Editor, Andy Serwer, at Fortune, and John Huey, when he was trying to kill a story that you may have worked on at Fortune about his cancer treatment and everything else.

And he finally said, "What do you have in the story?" And Serwer told him what's in the book. And he finally said, "Well, wait a minute, you've discovered that I'm an asshole? Why is that news?" So, he was self-aware, he was tough.

Source: Walter Isaacson interview, Fortune, Dec 27, 2011

183. Gorilla Glass

"This is what I want, a glass that can do this." So, Wendell Weeks says, "We once created a type of process that created something called Gorilla Glass." And Steve said,

"No, no, no. Here's how you make really strong glass."
And Wendell says, "Wait a minute, I know how to make
glass. Shut up and listen to me." And Steve, to his
credit, shuts up and listens, and Wendell Weeks
describes a process that makes Gorilla Glass. And
Steve then says, "Fine. In six months I want enough of
it to make--whatever it is—a million iPhones." And
Wendell says, "I'm sorry, we've actually never made it.
We don't have a factory to make it. This was a process
we developed, but we never had a manufacturing
plant to do it." And Steve looks at him and says what
he said to Woz, 20, 30 years earlier: "Don't be afraid,
you can do it." Wendell Weeks tells me... Because I
flew to Corning, because I just wanted to hear this
story. Wendell Weeks tells me, "I just sat there and
looked at the guy. He kept saying, 'Don't be afraid. You
can do this.'"

Source: Walter Isaacson interview, Fortune, Dec 27,
2011

184. Logo

He's paid $100,000 to have the logo for NeXT Computer. Paul Rand, who did it, who was a great designer — [Steve Jobs] said, "I want you to design a business card for me." It was "Steven P. Jobs." And they fought over whether the period after the P should be under the P, which is what you could do with bitmap displays, or if it should be right afterward, which was the normal way of doing it. And they fought so badly that Paul Rand would not surrender, and Steve Jobs had it done his own way. This is the passion for detail and perfection that is usually considered a micromanaging passion, but he does connect it, too, to the broad vision. And the broad vision is... I mean, look, the whole desktop publishing industry comes out of the fact that he cared about fonts.

Source: Walter Isaacson interview, Fortune, Dec 27, 2011

185. Cover

"That is the ugliest thing — this has such poor taste," and it was actually words of one syllable that were stronger than that. "You shouldn't even come to the product launch, I never want to deal with you again. You have no taste," and whatever.

Finally, he says, "I'm only going to keep dealing with you if you let me have some input into the cover." "Because," he said, "nobody is going to read your book, I'm not going to read your book. But I'll look at the cover — and I don't want it to be ugly." Now, it takes me about one and a half seconds to say, "Sure!" I mean, here's a guy with the greatest design eye of our time. That is basically Steve Jobs saying, "That's what the cover should look like." With a font that comes from the original Mac, the sans serif font, and the Albert Watson picture, and it's in black and white. And I said, "Shouldn't we do it in color?" He says, "No, I'm a black and white sort of guy: Things are either black, or they're white. It's a black and white cover."

Source: Walter Isaacson interview, Fortune, Dec 27, 2011

186. IMac name

Jobs said the new computer was a Mac, so the name had to reference the Macintosh brand. The name had to make it clear the machine was designed for the internet. It also had to be applicable to several other upcoming products. And it had to be quick: the packaging needed to be ready in a week.

iMac. "It referenced the Mac, and the "i" meant internet," Segall says. "But it also meant individual, imaginative and all the other things it came to stand for." The "i" prefix could also be applied to whatever other internet products Apple was working on. Jobs rejected them all, including iMac.

"He didn't like iMac when he saw it," Segall says. "I personally liked it, so I went back again with three or four new names, but I said we still like "iMac." He said: 'I don't hate it this week, but I still don't like it.'"

Segall didn't hear any more about the name from Jobs personally, but friends told him that Jobs was silk-screening the name on prototypes of the new computer. He was testing it out to see if it looked good. "He rejected it twice but then it just appeared on the machine," Segall says, laughing. "He never formally accepted it."

Source: Ken Segall interview, Cult of Mac, Nov 3, 2009

187. Family screening

Jobs and his kids sat down for their first family screening of Pixar's 2004 release "The Incredible's." After that, he tracked the countdown to the 100 millionth song sold on the iTunes store. Apple had promised a prize to the person who moved the odometer to 10 figures, and as the big number approached, fortune seekers snapped up files at a furious rate. At around 10:15, 20-year-old Kevin Britten of Hays, Kans., bought a song by the electronica band Zero 7, and Jobs himself got on the phone to tell him that he'd won. Then Jobs asked a potentially embarrassing question:

"Do you have a Mac or PC?"

"I have a Macintosh... duh!" said Britten.

Jobs laughs while recounting this.

Source: Newsweek, Jul 25, 2004

188. Autographs

"I hear you're not really one to give autographs, but I just gotta ask....will you sign my iPod? It's fine if you don't want to. I'm not normally one to even ask for autographs".

Steve: *chuckling* "it's quite alright. You heard that about me?? well I wouldn't say that I don't like giving autographs, I guess I was never comfortable with the idea solely taking credit for something, which is to me what an autograph might imply. To be honest, I think I'm the last person who should sign something. A writer signing a book I can understand, but I think if anybody within our company should sign something, it should be members from our R&D team and all the others responsible for product innovation. It's unfortunate that they all can't receive the same level recognition. But I suppose it's easier this way though?... you would need a pretty big iPod to fit all those signatures".

Source: Mac Rumors, Dec 19, 2011

189. Mayer

Mayer was offered an offer he couldn't turn down from RIM who wanted to sponsor his Summer tour. Mayer had no reservations about saying yes but decided to give Jobs a call just to give him a quick heads up and let him know that the RIM contract would require him to use RIM products exclusively. Thankfully for him RIM only made smart phones!

So Mayer calls up Jobs who, believe it or not, praises RIM for the work they do and casually mentions that he'll send Mayer an iPhone "to at least play with on the bus."

"I accepted the offer with Blackberry, and in the months leading up to the July 29th release date, the iPhone became the most desired item on the planet. Everybody wanted one, and nobody had yet to see one in person. It was mythical. That day I was playing an amphitheatre in Indianapolis, and sometime in the afternoon the production office got a call over the radio that a sales associate from the local Apple Store was standing at the outermost gate of the venue with something addressed to me. A few minutes later someone knocked on my dressing room door and handed me an Apple Store bag. Inside was an iPhone, and taped to it was a card; it belonged to Steve Jobs, CEO, 1 Infinite Loop, Cupertino, California. Handwritten on the backside of the card was one word: 'Enjoy!'"

Source: Edible Apple, Oct 20, 2011

190. Rainy Sunday

Several months later, on a rainy Sunday afternoon, I got a call. It went exactly like this:

"Hello?"

"Hello. May I speak with Lucas Haley?"

"Speaking."

"Hi. This is Steve Jobs."

At this point I was ready to call bull on whichever friend was prank calling me. I barely caught myself in time, remembering that I hadn't told anyone about the letter. This couldn't be anyone but Steve Jobs. The sudden realisation strengthened my suspicion that I hadn't said anything in an awkwardly long time, and I blurted out a weak "Can ... can I help you?"

Steve Jobs and I spoke on the phone that afternoon for over 20 minutes, about college, about work, about chasing dreams, and about how he couldn't give me a job but here's the name of someone who could. It was all very surreal, and immediately upon hanging up it felt like it couldn't have happened.

Source: Lucas Haley, FOX News, Oct 6, 2011

191. Three dot

Steve had no idea who Herb Caen was, much less the tremendous clout he had with hundreds of thousands of Bay Area followers who religiously read his "Baghdad by the Bay" daily columns. One mention in one of Herb's "three dot" columns could make or break your social life or even your career. So, I introduced Steve to Herb.

Herb said, "It's a great pleasure to meet you at last," and Steve's only reply was, "how come the Chronicle is such a bad newspaper?"

"It used to be a good paper," Herb said with a twinkle in his eyes. "Why, what would you consider a good newspaper?"

This certainly got Will Hearst attention. "Hopefully, the Examiner," he laughed.

"I only read the San Jose Mercury," Steve said. "It covers the greatest industry in the Universe like no one else."

"But Steve," Will interjected, "The Mercury is in Silicon Valley so of course they cover technology more."

Source: David Bunnell, Cult of Mac, May 4, 2010

192. Photographers

Steve didn't like the images we had chosen for the Mac screens. Aware that he might bolt any moment, Andrew and I worked feverishly to fix them — putting up exactly what Steve said he wanted. Meanwhile he stared at Mosgrove, and said, "Are you one of those type of photographers who takes dozens of photos hoping one of them will turn out okay?" Will just looked at him and shrugged.

"Take a picture of this," Steve said, holding up his middle finger. We stared in disbelief. Someone must have keyed his Mercedes again, I remember thinking.

Crazy as it was, the "computer gods" were with us that day. Somehow we got our Steve Jobs photo and it is a classic, but if I wasn't a nimble thinker it would never have appeared. A couple weeks after the photo shoot, Steve called to say, "Gee, David, I've changed my mind, I don't want to be on the cover of Macworld."

"Too late," I lied, "the cover is already at the printer and we can't change it."

In reality, a few pages were at the printer, but not the cover, and we could have changed it if we really wanted to, which, of course, we didn't.

Source: David Bunnell, Cult of Mac, Apr 26, 2010

193. Backyard pool party

I first met Steve years ago at a backyard pool party. I was so flummoxed by the off chance I was breathing in his DNA, I could barely say a word. I am sure I made a winning first impression as I stumbled over my own name when we were introduced. I watched as he swam in the pool with his son. He seemed like a regular guy, a good dad having fun with his kids.

The next time I met him was when our children attended school together. He sat in on back-to-school night listening to the teacher drone on about the value of education (wait, isn't he one of those high-tech gods who didn't even graduate from college?) while the rest of us sat around pretending having Steve Jobs in the room was totally normal.

[...] It was at Halloween not long after when I realised he actually knew my name (yes, my name!). He and his wife put on a darn scary haunted house [...]. He was sitting on the walkway, dressed like Frankenstein. As I walked by with my son, Steve smiled and said, "Hi Lisen." My son thought I was the coolest mom in town when he realised The Steve Jobs knew me. Thanks for the coolness points, Steve.

Source: Lisen Stromberg, Aug 29, 2011

194.Beer-and-food event

Steve J. gave a beer-and-food event at Apple today to celebrate the new Chiat-Day ad campaign. As part of his praise for the new ad and its theme, "Think Different", he read a letter written by the mother of a child that was "different" regarding her child's response to the ad. It was a really lovely letter - brought tears to my eyes. If you can, you should get a copy of the letter and post it. The letter was initially sent to someone at Chiat-Day. (The food was, notably, all vegan).

Steve said that the feedback on the ad was about 75% favourable. The other 25% of negative reactions to the ad had that "come on, let's show 'em why we kick Microsoft's butt!" flavour. Steve said that back when we DID kick Microsoft (DOS's) butt by about a factor of 100, this was easy to do. Only took 15...30...maybe 60 seconds at the most to convey that message. Now that we only kick Microsoft's butt by a factor of 2 (or thereabouts), this is not a good strategy because it's much harder to convince people of that difference that quickly. Rather, we should adopt the techniques of someone like Nike.

Source: Dave Winer, Sep 30, 1997

195. Photo

Steve Jobs, walking with the usual spring in his step that never seemed to go away even as he started looking more frail. Bumping into Steve was a surprisingly common occurrence for such a large company as Apple.

Steve was heading towards a car parked next to the curb with its door open, waiting for him. The car was idling. A family was standing near the Apple sign outside the building, a common site for people to take photos on their pilgrimages to Apple.

The father turned to Steve as he passed close by and asked, "Excuse me, sir, would you mind taking our photo?" Steve paused for a moment as an iPhone was extended to him, realising that they didn't seem to know who he was. With a hint of enthusiasm, he said "Sure!" as he took the iPhone into his hands.

Steve took a great deal of care composing the photo, backing up a few steps several times, tapping the iPhone screen to lock focus, then said "Smile!" as he snapped the photo, grinning a little bit himself to encourage the family to follow suit.

Source: Chris Hynes, Oct 7, 2011

196. Presentation

Jobs pulled back a sheet that had covered an elliptical object on the conference table. The first new product on his grid: the iMac. It was a weird, egg-shaped beast but disarmingly attractive. Like all great Steve Jobs products, it had a human feel to it. You wanted to touch it. Its plastic case was a feel-good shade of fruity blue. During its development the informal code names for the project had been the names of Columbus's ships: Nina, Pinta, Santa Maria. Why? "A new world," he explained.

After putting the machine through its paces, he bore down on me. "Isn't that just great?" he asked, with the pride of a very pushy parent. Yes, I agreed, it's really neat. "It's not just 'neat'," he corrected me. "It's fucking fantastic."

Source: The Perfect Thing by Steven Levy

197. Unapologetic

unapologetic about the incompatibility [between iPod and other music software than iTunes], insisting that Apple should not make iPods interoperable with competitors until its customer demand it. I once tried to get him to admit that the limitation was unfriendly to customers, but he would not bulge. He challenged me to provide an example where Apple's actions could harm a listener. Finally I came up with something.

"You love Bob Dylan, Steve," I said. "He records with Sony, your competitor in selling music. What if Sony sold a really great, previously unreleased Dylan song on its music store? None of your iTunes customers could download it and listen to it on their computers or iPods. Isn't that a disadvantage?"

"Bob Dylan loves us," said Jobs. "He's never do that."

I thought that was a fairly lame comeback. But a few months later, Dylan did okay the release of two fantastic out takes from the legendary Blood on the Tracks sessions for online sale —on the iTunes store, not his own label Sony's store.

Source: The Perfect Thing by Steven Levy

198. Apple Market

On January 13, 2006, something interesting came to Job's attention. At Wall Street's close on that Friday afternoon, Apple's market capitalisation had reached $72.13 billion. what made it a milestone to Jobs was that the cap of Dell computers at that moment was $71.97 billion — almost a million dollars less. Recalling Dell's advice almost a decade earlier, the Apple CEO was moved to send out a company wide e-mail. "Team," he wrote his employees, "it turned out that Michael Dell wasn't perfect at predicting the future."

Source: The Perfect Thing by Steven Levy

199. Apple 100

Periodic meeting of what he calls the Apple 100. Ever the elitist, he describes those invited as not the highest-ranking executives on the organisational charts but the really key people, the people, he says, who you'd take on the life raft with you when the ship was sinking (presumably everyone else would go down in the drink). "I usually get up in the beginning," Jobs says, "and say something like 'Our revenues have doubled in the last two years. And our stock price is high and our shareholders are happy. And a lot of people think it's really great, we've got a lot to lose, let's play it safe. That's the most dangerous thing we can do. We have to get bolder, because we have world-class competitors now and we just can't stand still'."

Then Steve Jobs told the hundred what he intended to do. Even though Apple had created one of the most successful consumer electronic products in history and the most popular of those was the tiny iPod mini, he was going to pull the plug on it and make something better."We are going to redefine the whole industry," he told his people. "By coming up with a player that's a full-featured iPod, color display, a click wheel, dock connector, photos, everything — at a size that completely changes the rules."

Source: The Perfect Thing by Steven Levy

143

200. Apologise

I went over to shake [Steve Jobs]'s hand and apologise for the mix up [relative to En gadget posting an incorrect story about an iPhone delay].

His reaction completely threw me. I expected some of the chiding he was infamous for giving journalists, but I heard not even a hint of frustration. Actually, he just acted as though he had no idea what I was talking about. Like it had never happened. Seriously. This was probably the most unexpected reaction I could have possibly imagined -- I was completely flummoxed. Of course, I realised moments later he was snowing me big time, and that it was classic Steve passive-aggressive. But you're Steve Jobs, and it's lunch time, and what happened happened, so what exactly DO you say to that whole thing, right?

Well, my nemesis (and one of my best pals) Brian Lam notices Steve and I interacting, so he rolls over to say hello as well. No sooner than Brian introduces himself, Steve is telling him him all about how Gizmodo is his favourite tech blog, and how it's the first site he reads and that he put it above En gadget (motioning upwards with his finger). Ouch.

Source: Ryan Block, gdgt, Aug 26, 2011

201. Book

When the book was finished, Steve asked for a pre-release copy, which I duly sent.

At the time, all sorts of people were telling me that I needed to put quotes on the back cover of the book. So I asked Steve Jobs if he'd give me one. Various questions came back. But eventually Steve said, "Isaac Newton didn't have back-cover quotes; why do you want them?"

And that's how, at the last minute, the back cover of A New Kind of Science ended up with just a simple and elegant array of pictures. Another contribution from Steve Jobs, that I notice every time I look at my big book.

Source: Stephen Wolfram, Oct 6, 2011

202. Fruitarian

Jobs was a fruitarian (someone who only eats fruit), and he continued to be a strict vegan throughout his life. But he made an exception for Japanese food.

Such was his love of soba that he sent the chef from Café Mac, the Apple company cafeteria, to study at the Tsukiji Soba Academy and had him serve a dish called "sashimi soba," an original Steve Jobs creation.

Source: Hayashi Nobuyuki, Dec 2011

203. Meeting Obama

Jobs, who was known for his prickly, stubborn personality, almost missed meeting President Obama in the fall of 2010 because he insisted that the president personally ask him for a meeting. Though his wife told him that Obama "was really psyched to meet with you," Jobs insisted on the personal invitation, and the stand off lasted for five days. When he finally relented and they met at the Westin San Francisco Airport, Jobs was characteristically blunt. He seemed to have transformed from a liberal into a conservative.

"You're headed for a one-term presidency," he told Obama at the start of their meeting, insisting that the administration needed to be more business-friendly. As an example, Jobs described the ease with which companies can build factories in China compared to the United States, where "regulations and unnecessary costs" make it difficult for them. Jobs also criticised America's education system, saying it was "crippled by union work rules," noted Isaacson.

Jobs suggested that Obama meet six or seven other CEOs who could express the needs of innovative businesses -- but when White House aides added more names to the list, Jobs insisted that it was growing too big and that "he had no intention of coming." In preparation for the dinner, Jobs exhibited his notorious attention to detail, telling venture capitalist John Doerr that the menu of shrimp, cod and lentil salad was "far too fancy" and objecting to a chocolate truffle dessert. But he was overruled by the White House, which cited the president's fondness for cream pie.

Source: Huffington Post, Oct 20, 2011

204. New baby

[Steve Jobs is] rehearsing the roll out that will introduce his new baby, the NeXT computer, to the world. Dressed in blue jeans and a red flannel shirt, Jobs paces back and forth, reading lines into a wireless microphone. [...]. When the first slide appears on the screen, Jobs enthuses: "I really like that green." Around him, other NeXT executives chime in: "Great green. Great green".

The computer goes through its paces, playing music with the sound of a live orchestra, pulling up images as clear as photographs, retrieving quotes from a memory bank big enough to hold a bookshelf full of classics. Then a software glitch makes the image on the sleek black monitor freeze. NeXT employees tense up, expecting an infamous Jobs outburst. Jobs just stares at the screen, then shrugs. "We're hosed," he says calmly. "We'll fix that. No problem."

Later, a video shows the automated assembly plant that Jobs has built to manufacture the NeXT machines. Wandering back to sit with a handful of employees, Jobs watches as robot hands install the state-of-the-art chips that will power the computer. For a second he looks almost teary. "It's beautiful," he says softly.

Source: Newsweek, Oct 24, 1988

205. Birthday party

I met Jobs at a celebrity-filled birthday party for a youngster in New York City. As the evening progressed, I wandered around to discover that Jobs had gone off with the nine- year-old birthday boy to give him the gift he'd brought from California: a Macintosh computer. As I watched, he showed the boy how to sketch with the machine's graphics program. Two other party guests wandered into the room and looked over Job's shoulder. 'Hmmm,' said the first, Andy Warhol. 'What is this? Look at this, Keith. This is incredible!' The second guest, Keith Haring, the graffiti artist whose work now commands huge prices, went over. Warhol and Haring asked to take a turn at the Mac, and as I walked away, Warhol had just sat down to manipulate the mouse. 'My God!' he was saying, 'I drew a circle!'

But more revealing was the scene after the party. Well after the other guests had gone, Jobs stayed to tutor the boy on the fine points of using the Mac. Later, I asked him why he had seemed happier with the boy than with the two famous artists. His answer seemed unrehearsed to me: "Older people sit down and ask, 'What is it?' but the boy asks, 'What can I do with it?'"

Source: Playboy, Feb 1985

206. Ruthless

Jobs could be ruthless when he talked to the labels. Kevin Gage, then Warner's technology vice president, remembers one key meeting at Apple's Cupertino, California headquarters where he and Vidich tried to persuade Jobs that digital rights management – virtual "locks" to prevent songs from being shared – was necessary to get other labels on board.

He was three slides into a PowerPoint presentation when Jobs, rocking in his chair, exploded into a tirade about how the music business just didn't get it. "He said, 'You've got your head stuck up your ass' to me a number of times," Gage recalls. "There's that side of Steve – but in a smooth kind of way. He never reacted to Roger [Ames, then Warner's CEO] the same way he reacted to Paul and myself, put it that way. When Roger came into the room, you saw Steve at his brightest and sharpest."

Source: Rolling Stone, Oct 7, 2011

207. Come back

"Apple has already come back," and now that his days are not so intently involved in crisis management, and he is able to spend more time with his family, he appears to be having a wonderful time.

He runs Apple in a mode that can only be described as post-CEO. Sometimes he will greet visitors in shorts, sandals and a two-day beard growth. His office is a surprisingly compact rectangle cluttered with books, videos and advertising awards. On the phone, sitting at a desk that sports both Mac and Windows laptops [running NeXTSTEP], he schmoozes and deals with everyone from Pixar executives to Jerry Seinfeld, concerning Apple's ad on the Final Episode.

Last week he spent an extraordinary amount of time monitoring every last detail of the iMac intro; a typical executive decision was the elimination of a clarinet on a video soundtrack because it sounded "too synthetic."

Source: Newsweek, May 18, 1998

208. Interim CEO

I remember being at a talk he gave shortly after returning in 1997 as Interim CEO. A bunch of us employees (I was at ATG at the time) were in Town Hall in Building 4 at Infinite Loop to hear him, and he was fired up. Talked a lot about how Apple was going to completely turn things around and become great.

It was a tough time at Apple — we were trading below book value on the market — our enterprise value was actually less than our cash on hand. And the rumours were everywhere that we were going to be acquired by Sun. Someone in the audience asked him about Michael Dell's suggestion in the press a few days previous that Apple should just shut down and return the cash to shareholders, and as I recall, Steve's response was: "Fuck Michael Dell." Good god, what a message from a CEO!

He followed it up by admitting that the stock price was terrible (it was under $10, I think — pretty sure it was under $2 split-adjusted), and that what they were going to do was reissue everyone's options on the low price, but with a new 3 year vest. He said, explicitly: "If you want to make Apple great again, let's get going. If not, get the hell out." I think it's not an overstatement to say that just about everyone in the room loved him at that point, would have followed him off a cliff if that's where he led.

Source: John Lilly, Oct 9, 2011

209. Leakiest organisation

One of the struggles we were going through when he came back was that Apple was about the leakiest organisation in history — it had gotten so bad that people were cavalier about it. In the face of all those leaks, I remember the first all company e-mail that Steve sent around after becoming Interim CEO again — he talked in it about how Apple would release a few things in the coming week, and a desire to tighten up communications so that employees would know more about what was going on — and how that required more respect for confidentiality. That mail was sent on a Thursday; I remember all of us getting to work on Monday morning and reading mail from Fred Anderson, our then-CFO, who said basically: "Steve sent mail last week, he told you not to leak, we were tracking everyone's mail, and 4 people sent the details to outsiders. They've all been terminated and are no longer with the company." Well. If it wasn't clear before that the Amelio/Spindler/Sculley days of Apple were over, it was crystal clear then, and good riddance.

Source: John Lilly, Oct 9, 2011

210. Apple Computer's boardroom

Early on a July workday in 1997, Jim McCluney, then head of Apple's worldwide operations got the call. McCluney was summoned with other top brass of the beleaguered company to Apple Computer's boardroom on its Cupertino campus. Embattled Chief Executive Gil Amelio wasted no time. With an air of barely concealed relief, he said: "Well, I'm sad to report that it's time for me to move on. Take care," McCluney recalls. And he left.

A few minutes later, in walked Steve Jobs. The co-founder of the once proud company had been fired by Apple 12 years before. He had returned seven months earlier as a consultant, when Amelio acquired his NeXT Software. And now Jobs was back in charge. Wearing shorts, sneakers, and a few days' growth of beard, he sat down in a swivel chair and spun slowly, says McCluney, now president of storage provider Emulex. "O.K., tell me what's wrong with this place," Jobs said. After some mumbled replies, he jumped in: "It's the products! So what's wrong with the products?" Again, executives began offering some answers. Jobs cut them off. "The products suck!" he roared.

"There's no sex in them any more!"

Source: Business Week, Jan 26, 2006

211. Journalists

I was among the few journalists who got to test [the iPhone] before its release. Soon after I received the unit, I was walking down Broadway and my test unit got a call from "Unknown." It was Jobs, ostensibly wanting to know what I thought, but actually making sure I understood how amazing it was. I acknowledged that it was extraordinary, but mentioned to him that maybe nothing could match the expectations he had generated. People were calling it the "Jesus phone." Didn't that worry him? The answer was no. "We are going to blow away the expectations," he told me.

Source: Steven Levy, Wired, Oct 5, 2011

212. San Francisco party

Anyone who doubts the tenacity of Steven P. Jobs gets an earful from his head cheerleader and principal investor, billionaire H. Ross Perot. Perot tells of a San Francisco party last year where he ran into the King of Spain. When the King asked whom else he should meet there, Perot suggested Jobs. Soon, the King engaged the entrepreneur in what Perot recalls as an "electric conversation," with Jobs gesturing madly in front of the transfixed monarch. Then the King took out his card, scribbled on the back, and handed it to Jobs. Perot hurried across the room. "What happened?" Replied a beaming Jobs: "I sold him a computer."

Source: Business Week, Oct 24, 1988

213. Cube's

Job's nagging perfectionism extended to every detail. He insisted on a finish inside the [NeXT] cube's magnesium shell -- even though it would never be seen.

He disliked a tiny line left in the chassis by the molds for the cube, a flaw most computer makers deem unavoidable. Jobs flew to Chicago to persuade the die caster to retool. "Not a lot of die casters expect a celebrity to fly in," says Kelley.

Source: Business Week, Oct 24, 1988

214. Calla lily

Jobs had to have a calla lily. It was 11 p.m in New York City in December 1983, and he absolutely had to have a calla lily in his suite at the Carlyle Hotel. No other flower would do. He also needed a piano. "Not that he played one," says Andrea Cunningham, who did marketing for Apple. He merely stipulated that his room have one. Cunningham was part of Job's entourage in town for a Fortune magazine photo shoot to promote the Mac, which was going to be introduced just a month later on Jan. 24, 1984.

"He was being such a pill," says Cunningham. "He staunchly refused to do anything the photographer asked." To lighten the mood, she set up a tape recorder and played music Jobs liked—the Michael Jackson album Thriller. No dice; Jobs refused to pose. Then the song Billie Jean came on. "He snapped to and was a different guy," she says. "And as soon as the song ended, he reverted back. So I kept rewinding the tape to play over and over so he'd behave."

Source: Business Week, Oct 6, 2011

215. Logo

If Jobs knew NeXT was a loser, he rarely let on. He remained demanding, confident, and grandiose.

Asked to deliver the keynote speech at a computer trade show at the Javits Convention Center in Manhattan, Jobs told MacAskill to ship out Job's own desk—complete with the vase and red rose he always kept there—for him to sit at on stage. He insisted that the desk be placed at a 28-degree angle, to match the angle of Rand's box-shaped logo, which was tipped to one side.

A few minutes before the curtains opened, MacAskill begged Jobs not to introduce a new Lotus spreadsheet that hadn't been cleared by Lotus. "Fine," Jobs said, "then you do the speech," and walked off "only to return as the curtain opened." MacAskill says he and everyone else put up with the volatility and withering personal insults because "we really thought we had the chance to change the world."

Source: Business Week, Oct 6, 2011

216. Chief James

A few months after taking over, Jobs called operations chief James M. McCluney and hardware engineering chief Rubinstein into his office and dramatically lifted a Styrofoam model of what would be the iMac out of a bowling bag. The duo reported back a few weeks later that it wouldn't work, because they couldn't find room for a floppy drive. Hardly missing a beat, Jobs said, "No worries. Disk drives are over the hill. CDs are going to get so cheap that no one will miss [floppies]." Says McCluney: "It was remarkable. It was a snap judgement."

Source: Business Week, Oct 6, 2011

217. Layout

On my first day at NeXT, as we walked around the building, my colleagues shared in hushed voices that Jobs personally chose the wood flooring and various appointments. He even specified the outdoor sprinkler system layout.

I witnessed his attention to detail during a marketing reorganisation meeting. The VP of marketing read Jobs's e-mailed reaction to the new org chart. Jobs simply requested that the charts be reprinted with the official corporate blue and green colors. Shifted color space was like a horribly distorted concerto to his senses.

Source: Steve Jurvetson on Steve Jobs, Business Week, Oct 6, 2011

218. Call

I never knew when Steve was going to call. But I knew that when he did, it would probably be in the middle of the night.

In 2001 my company was developing Ethernet chips for Mac computers. Steve was enormously excited about our product. He was enormously excited about everything. And restless and sometimes agitated—and frankly, he could be a bit of a pain. He was like a bulldog. He worked all the time, day and night, and he expected everyone around him to be that way, too. He insisted that the person at the top or someone who had absolute control was the guy he interfaced with. He demanded that he get as much time as necessary.

If it was 3 in the morning and Steve had a thought or a question or complaint, he picked up the phone and called, right then. The concept of "that can wait until the morning" did not apply. He wasn't going to sleep until he addressed the issue.

Source: Henry Nicholas, Business Week, Oct 6, 2011

219. 72 sleepless

I worked at one point for 72 sleepless hours for something that Steve Jobs showed on stage for 9 seconds. It's top three, if not No. 1, of my professional achievements. It didn't look any different on that screen as it did on mine, but it was the knowledge that it was good enough to be on the stage that made it suddenly look different. I'll never get that chance again, and I'm glad I had it.

Source: Matt Drance, Business Week, Oct 6, 2011

220. Nike+

We had worked together on a Nike-Apple collaboration called Nike+. So we took what Apple knows and Nike knows, and brought new technology to the market. Anyway, long story short, he said, "Congratulations. It's great [that you've been named CEO]. You're going to do a great job." I said, "Well, do you have any advice?"

He said, "No, no, you're great." Then there was a pause. "Well, I do have some advice," he said. "Nike makes some of the best products in the world--products that you lust after, absolutely beautiful stunning products. But you also make a lot of crap."

He said, "Just get rid of the crappy stuff, and focus on the good stuff." And then I expected a little pause and a laugh. But there was a pause, and no laugh at the end.

Source: Mark Parker, president and CEO of Nike

221. Think Different

Jobs was quiet during the pitch [of the Think Different campaign by TBWA], but he seemed intrigued throughout, and now it was time for him to talk.

He looked around the room filled with the "Think Different" billboards and said, "This is great, this is really great ... but I can't do this. People already think I'm an egotist, and putting the Apple logo up there with all these geniuses will get me skewered by the press."

The room was totally silent. The "Think Different" campaign was the only campaign we had in our bag of tricks, and I thought for certain we were toast.

Steve then paused and looked around the room and said out loud, yet almost as if to his own self, "What am I doing? Screw it. It's the right thing. It's great. Let's talk tomorrow." In a matter of seconds, right before our very eyes, he had done a complete about-face.

Source: Fordbes, Dec 14, 2011

222. No overcoat

One frigid winter day in the late 1970s, I ran into Steve at some meeting in mid town Manhattan, a time and event now long forgotten. What isn't forgotten is that when the meeting ended and we went outside into the freezing weather, I was reasonably comfortable in my wool overcoat, but Steve was freezing. No overcoat, not even a jacket.

I suggested that he buy a coat. He agreed. So off we went to Paul Stuart, my favourite men's store, just a few blocks away on Madison Avenue. After quickly trying on a few, he picked one. He then asked the salesman the price. Oops.

"That much for an overcoat? Too much. Besides, I'll never use it in California."

We left the store. I in my overcoat, warm. Steve coat less, freezing.

223. Conferences

The Western Electronic Manufacturers Association used to hold annual industry conferences in Monterey. Steve keynoted one of the conferences in the early 1980s. But rather than tout the greatness of Apple, or the potential of personal computers, or anything material or mundane, Steve spoke passionately for 40 minutes on one subject -- the dangers of nuclear warfare. That was it.

The audience, needless to say, was dumbfounded. Steve spoke, took no questions, and sat down. Steve, it turns out, had a lot of passions.

Source: Ben Rosen, Oct 22, 2011

224. Sunday morning

One Sunday morning, January 6th, 2008 I was attending religious services when my cell phone vibrated. As discreetly as possible, I checked the phone and noticed that my phone said "Caller ID unknown". I choose to ignore.

After services, as I was walking to my car with my family, I checked my cell phone messages. The message left was from Steve Jobs. "Vic, can you call me at home? I have something urgent to discuss" it said. Before I even reached my car, I called Steve Jobs back. I was responsible for all mobile applications at Google, and in that role, had regular dealings with Steve. It was one of the perks of the job.

"Hey Steve - this is Vic", I said. "I'm sorry I didn't answer your call earlier. I was in religious services, and the caller ID said unknown, so I didn't pick up". Steve laughed. He said, "Vic, unless the Caller ID said 'GOD', you should never pick up during services". I laughed nervously. [...]

"So Vic, we have an urgent issue, one that I need addressed right away. I've already assigned someone from my team to help you, and I hope you can fix this tomorrow" said Steve. "I've been looking at the Google logo on the iPhone and I'm not happy with the icon. The second O in Google doesn't have the right yellow gradient. It's just wrong and I'm going to have Greg fix it tomorrow. Is that okay with you?" Of course this was okay with me. A few minutes later on that Sunday I received an email from Steve with the subject "Icon Ambulance". The email directed me to work with Greg Christie to fix the icon.

Source: Vic Gundotra, Google+, Aug 25, 2011

225. Tech conference

To my knowledge, the only tech conference Steve Jobs regularly appeared at, the only event he didn't somehow control, was our D: All Things Digital conference, where he appeared repeatedly for unrehearsed, on stage interviews. We had one rule that really bothered him: We never allowed slides, which were his main presentation tool.

One year, about an hour before his appearance, I was informed that he was backstage preparing dozens of slides, even though I had reminded him a week earlier of the no- slides policy. I asked two of his top aides to tell him he couldn't use the slides, but they each said they couldn't do it, that I had to. So, I went backstage and told him the slides were out. Famously prickly, he could have stormed out, refused to go on. And he did try to argue with me. But, when I insisted, he just said "Okay." And he went on stage without them, and was, as usual, the audience's favourite speaker.

Source: Walt Mossberg, Oct 5, 2011

226. Fifth D

For our fifth D conference, both Steve and his long time rival, the brilliant Bill Gates, surprisingly agreed to a joint appearance, their first extended on stage joint interview ever. But it almost got derailed.

Earlier in the day, before Gates arrived, I did a solo on stage interview with Jobs, and asked him what it was like to be a major Windows developer, since Apple's iTunes program was by then installed on hundreds of millions of Windows PCs. He quipped:

"It's like giving a glass of ice water to someone in Hell."

When Gates later arrived and heard about the comment, he was, naturally, enraged, because my partner Kara Swisher and I had assured both men that we hoped to keep the joint session on a high plane.

In a pre-interview meeting, Gates said to Jobs: "So I guess I'm the representative from Hell." Jobs merely handed Gates a cold bottle of water he was carrying. The tension was broken, and the interview was a triumph, with both men acting like statesmen. When it was over, the audience rose in a standing ovation, some of them in tears.

Source: Walt Mossberg, Oct 5, 2011

227. First retail store

Apple opened its first retail store [...] in the Washington, D.C., suburbs, near my home. [Steve Jobs] conducted a press tour for journalists, as proud of the store as a father is of his first child. I commented that, surely, there'd only be a few stores, and asked what Apple knew about retailing.

He looked at me like I was crazy, said there'd be many, many stores, and that the company had spent a year tweaking the layout of the stores, using a mock up at a secret location. I teased him by asking if he, personally, despite his hard duties as CEO, had approved tiny details like the translucency of the glass and the color of the wood. He said he had, of course.

Source: Walt Mossberg, Oct 5, 2011

228. Liver transplant

After his liver transplant, while he was recuperating at home in Palo Alto, California, Steve invited me over to catch up on industry events that had transpired during his illness. It turned into a three-hour visit, punctuated by a walk to a nearby park that he insisted we take, despite my nervousness about his frail condition.

He explained that he walked each day, and that each day he set a farther goal for himself, and that, today, the neighbourhood park was his goal. As we were walking and talking, he suddenly stopped, not looking well. I begged him to return to the house, noting that I didn't know CPR and could visualise the headline: "Helpless Reporter Lets Steve Jobs Die on the Side walk."

But he laughed, and refused, and, after a pause, kept heading for the park. We sat on a bench there, talking about life, our families, and our respective illnesses (I had had a heart attack some years earlier). He lectured me about staying healthy. And then we walked back.

Source: Walt Mossberg, Oct 5, 2011

229. Rebecc

Before I met the wife I had a girlfriend named Rebecca. Rebecca had non-Hodgkinsons lymphoma. It was a rough time in her life and she was very depressed by it, even though chemotherapy was healing her over time. Rebecca was a big fan of Pixar films.

[...] I sent a letter to Steve Jobs telling him about Rebecca and her situation. I asked for an autograph for her, hoping that could be something positive for her and encourage some positivity. I never thought I would get a reply, but i thought it was worth a try.

A week later I receive a package in the mail. In this thick envelope was a letter from

Steve Jobs speaking of his cancer fight and how he wished Rebecca a quick recovery. Also in this envelope was six Pixar prints signed by John Lasseter, Andrew Stanton, Mike Doctor, and Joe Ranft (a fellow cancer sufferer). Each of these men had written a letter to Rebecca wishing her well.

Source: Kristopher Wright, Quora, Oct 6, 2011

230. Genius

Steve Jobs was a genius, but he knew his limits. "He was never a guy who tried to make believe he had expertise in something," said Barry Schuler, now a partner at venture capital firm Draper Fisher Jurvetson. That was clear to Schuler when he got a call from Jobs in early 1997 to come over to his old offices at NeXT Software in Redwood City, Calif. Jobs, at that point, hadn't yet agreed to run Apple on a permanent basis.

"What's this Internet thing?" Schuler recalled Jobs asking. "I don't get it. What are people doing on it? What do they like about it?" Schuler, who was AOL's president of creative development at the time, remembered Jobs asking if the excitement was about reading magazines online.

"I don't get why anyone would want to read a magazine on a computer screen," he said. "That's a terrible experience."

Source: Business Week, Oct 12, 2011

231. Tension-free

Working with Jobs was far from tension-free. When the limestone that arrived in Cupertino didn't match the sample Jobs had approved, he called to yell at [architect Ronnette Riley] for not checking the shipment personally while in Italy.

Another time, she was whispering to someone in the corner of the conference room while Jobs was interrogating someone on the other side of the room.

"Suddenly, he turned around and said, 'Could you please be quiet—I'm trying to yell at someone over here!' " Riley said.

Source: Business Week, Oct 12, 2011

232. Two questions

One of my friends did an intern ship at Apple. Apparently Apple has a day where the interns get to meet Steve Jobs (this was obviously a few years back) and ask him questions. Two questions that were asked stuck in her mind:

1. "What do you wish for the most?" Steve Jobs: "I wish people would stop asking me stupid questions."

2. "What do you do in your free time?"

Steve Jobs: "I fuck my wife."

Source: Dan Zhang, Quora, Dec 29, 2011

233. Design for garden

In 1996, Steve Jobs and Penelope Hob house discussed her design for his garden. "He swept into the ... restaurant on his roller blades and sat down," she wrote. "I wish I had taped the conversation. ... I do recall the intensity of his beliefs."

Hob house was preparing for a three-week tour of the United States when she got an unexpected phone call from the Apple co-founder. "The man just said his name and that he'd like me to come and redesign his garden in Palo Alto, California," she wrote.

[...] "Mr. Jobs asked me to do an English cottage garden," she recalled - a perfect fit for his Tudor-style home on Waverley Street. "That was quite easy for me to do; the plants weren't a problem. It was a really nice project. He didn't know a lot about gardening but he knew the style he wanted. Later, we sent him pictures of every single plant we recommended.

"I was a great admirer of his, and appreciate his ideas about beauty and simplicity," Hob house continued. "He was rather wonderful. He didn't allow other people to have second-rate standards." In three days, she saw no hint of the Jobs that some associates described as "intimidating, demanding, ferocious, arrogant, intolerant, sometimes abusive, always obsessive about control." With her, he was "a nice courteous man."

Source: Joe Eaton and Ron Sullivan, SF Chronicle, Feb 2012

234. Tom Suiter

A good friend of mine, Tom Suiter, was a very good friend of Steve's. [...] Steve called him one day when he was starting NeXT — he had broken away from Apple and taken his people, and they were looking for a name for the company. He called him excitedly to say: "Hey Tom, I have this name I'm thinking of for my new company. I'm thinking of calling it Two."

Tom paused and said: "Well, I don't know about that, Steve. People might ask you about what happened to One." Then Steve said, "That's why I'm calling you. I think it's a good name, but if you've got a better one that'd be great, could you think about that?"

Later Tom found himself listening to a speech from Bill Gates. During the speech Bill Gates kept using the word "next" when he was talking about new technologies coming from Microsoft. He used the word often enough that Tom noted his repetition and thought, "Wait a minute: next, that means future, that's a cool thing." And the next day he called Steve and said, "I've got the name for you. Next." And there's that pause on the other end, where with Steve you never know what's going to come. It could be, "That's the stupidest thing I've ever heard," or it could be, "Great." And he says, "I love it!"

Source: Ken Segall on the name 'NeXT'

235. Lisa

Apparently, Jobs was asked to contribute an item to a time capsule that was being created in honour of the theme of that conference: "The Future Isn't What It Used to Be" (note: in Aspen in 1983). He looked around to find something to add:

After Steve Jobs' speech, in which he used an Apple Lisa computer to control what Celuch recalls was a 6 projector set up, John approached Jobs and asked for something that he could include in the time capsule.

Jobs thought about it for a few seconds and then unplugged the mouse from the Lisa. Celuch recalls that he was amused by the manner in which he was handed the mouse, as Jobs held the mouse by its cord, almost as one would hold a real mouse by the tail. So into the time capsule the Lisa mouse went, where it was buried at the end of the conference to be unearthed about 20 years later.

But that time capsule was never dug up and its location is now a mystery. The land changed hands, improvements were made and the capsule was lost.

Source: Matthew Panzarino, The Next Web, October 2012

236. Executive committee meeting

According to one person who attended an executive committee meeting soon after the Next acquisition, one item on the agenda was to discuss print advertising strategy for the then-newly released Macintosh 3400 and Power Mac machines. Amelio turned the meeting over to the company's vice president of advertising and brand communications, David Roman, who would unveil the "We're Back" series of ads, and urged the group to save their questions until after Roman was finished.

Roman had barely started when Jobs interrupted, clearly agitated. It was apparently something Roman said about placing Macintosh ads in newspapers. "Why do we want to spend all this money on newspaper advertising when these newspapers are killing us on the editorial page?" Jobs asked, as quoted by the person who attended the meeting.

[...]

"We were kind of stunned at how quickly Gil lost control of the meeting, about how he was unwilling to stand up to Jobs," said another Apple executive who also attended the meeting. [...] In the end, Amelio's cautious and non-confrontational style created an environment in which Jobs could freely impose his hyper-formidable will.

Source: The 'new' Jobs shows two faces, The San Jose Mercury News, August 10, 1997

237. Amelio

Since Amelio was forced to resign, Jobs has been a regular presence around Apple, patrolling the hallways and pop-quizzing employees on their work. And he has quickly added to his temperamental legend.

According to a person briefed about a recent meeting with Jobs, Jobs looked around the conference room, remarked that he "always hated this conference room," and moved the meeting to a new room. There, he grilled everyone in attendance about his or her role: When one person identified himself as a speech writer, Jobs shook his head, said, "No speech writer," and banished him from the meeting.

Source: The 'new' Jobs shows two faces, The San Jose Mercury News, August 10, 1997

238. Company was in trouble

Prior to his return to Apple, it was obvious that the company was in trouble. [...] I wrote an impassioned email to Steve at Pixar, pleading with him to find something else to do with his time. "Please," I implored him, "don't come back to Apple, you'll ruin it." At the time, I really thought Steve and Larry were just twisting the knife into an already struggling company. As I made my living on Macs, I wanted the company to survive and not be distracted by Steve and Larry's games.

Shortly thereafter, Steve emailed me. He explained what he was trying to do, and that he was trying to save Apple. And then he wrote the words I'll never forget: "You may be right. But if I succeed, remember to look in the mirror and call yourself an asshole for me."

Consider it done, Steve. I could not have been more mistaken.

Source: Michell Smith, Quora, Oct 24 2012

239. Contract recruiter

In 1988, I was self-employed as a recruiter and had referred a number of candidates to Steve at NeXT Computer, which he subsequently hired. I had also worked at Sun Micro systems as a contract recruiter. In September of that year, Steve invited me to his offices on Deer Creek Road in Palo Alto for an informal interview. He was 45 minutes late. As soon as Steve led me into his office and closed the door, he turned and said,

"You recruited for Sun and Sun hires shitty people."

"Well," I retorted, "You hired the ones Sun didn't want."

At that point, Steve cracked a big smile and exclaimed, "Touché!"

After that, we had a nice chat for about twenty minutes. During this time, a crowd of NeXT employees gathered and paced outside. When Steve opened the door to escort me out, he was mobbed like a celebrity, while I was shoved aside. As I was about to exit the lobby, I heard Steve call out my name. I turned and saw Steve bending down and waving to me, childlike. I walked away thinking to myself, "That guy can be a real jerk, but he sure is charming."

Source: Bill Lee, Quora, Dec 10 2012

240. Palo Alto

I bumped into Steve at the Palo Alto Whole Foods near both of our homes. He was in front of me in line paying for his groceries. It was the express checkout and he was wearing his traditional black turtle-neck. This was back in the early 2000s.

Here was a very wealthy, smart guy arguing with the cashier about what the correct change was for his purchase. He was demanding that he got another quarter ($0.25) for his change. This discussion went on for several minutes and held up the line so much that everyone behind him (including us) were getting annoyed. I guess Steve had to be right. The cashier gave him a quarter and he walked away.

Source: Roy Pereira, Quora, Oct 24 2012

241. Randy Adams

Software engineer Randy Adams initially turned down Steve Jobs' offer to work at NeXT, the computer company started by Jobs after his ouster from Apple. It was 1985. Adams wasn't ready to go back to work after selling his pioneering desktop software publishing company. Within a few days Jobs was on Adams' answering machine. "You're blowing it, Randy. This is the opportunity of a lifetime, and you're blowing it." Adams reconsidered.

Adams, using some of the cash he'd earned from the sale of his company, bought a Porsche 911 at the same time Jobs did. To avoid car-door dings, they parked near each other–taking up three parking spaces between them. One day Jobs rushed over to Adams' cubicle and told him they had to move the cars.

"I said, 'Why?,' and he said, 'Randy, we have to hide the Porsches. Ross Perot is coming by and thinking of investing in the company, and we don't want him to think we have a lot of money.'" They moved the cars around to the back of NeXT's offices in Palo Alto, Calif. and Perot invested $20 million in the company in 1987 and took a seat on the board.

Source: Randy Adams to Forbes, Oct 3 2012

242. Personal prototype iPhone

In the fall of 2006, my wife, Laura, and I went out to dinner with Steve and his brilliant and lovely wife, Laurene. Sitting outside of the restaurant on California Avenue in Palo Alto waiting for a table to open up, on a balmy Silicon Valley evening, Steve pulled his personal prototype iPhone out of his jeans pocket and said, 'Here, let me show you something.' He took me on a tour through all of the features and capabilities of the new device.

After an appropriate amount of oohing and aahing, I ventured a comment. BlackBerry aficionado as I was, I said, 'Boy, Steve, don't you think it's going to be a problem not having a physical keyboard? Are people really going to be okay typing directly on the screen?' He looked me right in the eye with that piercing gaze and said, 'They'll get used to it.'

Source: Marc Andreessen to Forbes, Oct 3 2012

243. Five iMacs

In 1998 my wife and I bought five iMacs as Christmas gifts for our grandchildren. We watched them open their presents, and when 5-year-old Molly opened her iMac, she said, 'Life is good.' Unfortunately, Molly's iMac developed a problem. After using it a few hours, the disc drive door would not open. The dealer told me he was not authorised to exchange the computer for another one due to an Apple policy. Repair would take several weeks, he told me.

I sent an e-mail to Steve and asked him about Apple's return/exchange policy on a new product. Within five minutes my phone rang. It was Steve. He asked me what the problem was and the name of the dealer. 'I'll call you back,' he said. A few minutes later the phone rang and it was a very apologetic dealer. 'I have a new iMac here for your granddaughter,' he said. I e-mailed Steve, thanking him and assuring him that he had made my granddaughter's Christmas a happy one. Steve immediately replied with a simple 'Ho, ho, ho.'

Source: Regis McKenna to Forbes, Oct 3 2012

244. iPhone announced

Shortly before Jobs and Apple unveiled the original iPhone at MacWorld in 2007, a group of engineers from the iPhone team went to Jobs' home to debug a problem with the phone's WiFi. At one point while the team was working, a FedEx employee buzzed outside the house to deliver a package to Jobs.

"Steve goes out to meet him because he has to sign for this package, but he's got the iPhone in one of his hands," said a former Apple employee was with the iPhone team at the time. "Steve just walks out casually, [hides] the phone behind his back, signs the package, and the FedEx dude marches off."

The idea that Jobs would walk outside carrying an iPhone in plain sight shocked this employee, given how much effort Apple put into keeping the product secret at all costs.

"You have to understand, when we carried the phones to his house, we carried them in these Pelican lock boxes. These phones were never to leave Apple's campus, and Steve just casually throws it behind his back. That was the first time I saw someone casually come close to seeing the iPhone before it was announced, and he didn't even know it. If the FexEx guy had just tilted his head, he would have seen it.

Source: Business Insider, July 27 2012

245. The Good Earth

In the early 1980s, Steve used to eat lunch at "The Good Earth", the now-defunct Cupertino restaurant where I waitresses when I was sixteen. I remember this nerdy young guy who always ordered the Good Earth tostada, served in a whole-wheat tortilla and topped with sprouts. He smiled shyly at me when he asked for more Good Earth tea and drank gallons of the stuff. Steve always sat alone, devouring books and manuals way beyond my limited teenage understanding along with his food. [...]

I called my mom the moment I heard Steve Jobs had died. She was sitting in front of her iMac, from which she has a view of the Cupertino Valley, The Apple headquarters nestled in the middle like a brilliant white palace. She was crying.

"There was a rainbow one day," she sobbed, "that ended right on top of Apple." My mom snapped a photograph. "I wanted to send it to him!" she added. "I meant to send it to him. And now," she stopped suddenly, struggling for control. "Now, he's dead."

Source: Suzanne, Oct 7 2011

246. CNBC

When CNBC reporter Jim Goldman interviewed Jobs after Tuesday's Macworld keynote, he passed on a comment from Robbie Bach, entertainment chief at Microsoft, that the Zune 2 is a "worthy alternative to Apple's iPod".

Jobs reply? "Was he inebriated? Do you even know anyone who owns a Zune?"

Source: Wired, Jan 18 2008

247. Apple and Pixar

Apple turns out many products--a dozen a year; if you count all the minor ones, probably a hundred. Pixar is striving to turn out one a year. But the converse of that is that Pixar's products will still be used fifty years from now, whereas I don't think you'll be using any product Apple brings to market this year fifty years from now. Pixar is making art for the ages. Kids will be watching Toy Story in the future. And Apple is much more of a constant race to continually improve things and stay ahead of the competition.

Name: Steve Jobs at 44 (Michael Krantz)

Published in: Time Magazine

Date: Oct 18, 1999

Source URL:
http://www.time.com/time/printout/0,8816,32207,00.html

248. Role At Pixar

Pixar my job is to help build the studio and recruit people and help create a situation where they can do the best work of their lives. And to some degree it's the same at Apple. But at Pixar, I don't direct the movies, whereas at Apple probably, if I had to pick a role out of a film production, I'd be the director. So it's a different job for me too, and I'm very conscious of that. My job at Pixar is to help manage the studio processes. But I don't say, "Well, I think we should have that character do that." I do give notes, just like other people do. There was one situation, for the first time, about three months ago, where I gave the best note. Which is really good, actually, because there were some very smart people there. But that will hardly ever happen.

Name: Steve Jobs at 44 (Michael Krantz)

Published in: Time Magazine

Date: Oct 18, 1999

Source URL:
http://www.time.com/time/printout/0,8816,32207,00.html

249. Product Lines

There were 15 product lines when I got here. It was incredible. You couldn"t figure out what to buy. I started asking around, and nobody could explain it to me. This year we updated the PowerBook, in May, the iBook in July, the G4, replacing the G3, in August at Seybold, and now the iMacs in October. I added up the time: in 148 days, we've completely changed every product. [He laughs.] We've been working too hard.

Name: Steve Jobs at 44 (Michael Krantz)

Published in: Time Magazine

Date: Oct 18, 1999

Source URL:
http://www.time.com/time/printout/0,8816,32207,00.html

250. Only Important Person

Both Pixar and Apple are team sports, even more so in my funny situation. I rely on a very great management team at Pixar because I'm not there all the time. I'm here [at Apple] a little more than I am there [at Pixar] these days. And without those folks, nothing of value would happen. I guess what I'm trying to say is, there's different things in life you can do. You can become a painter, you can become a sculptor. You can make something by yourself. But that's not what I do. I do the other thing, which is, you work at things that one person can't do, and that you need large numbers of people to do. I know people like symbols, but it's always unsettling when people write stories about me, because they tend to overlook a lot of other people.

Name: Steve Jobs at 44 (Michael Krantz)

Published in: Time Magazine

Date: Oct 18, 1999

Source URL:
http://www.time.com/time/printout/0,8816,32207,00.html

251. Broadband Web

I think there's a lot of possibility there, but there are a lot of problems between here and there. The Internet offers no guaranteed delivery. There's no guaranteed latency. You get a lot of traffic on that backbone, you have all sorts of problems. When you try to start moving huge amounts of information around with big high-fidelity images, there's just a lot of problems there. But they will get solved.

Name: Steve Jobs at 44 (Michael Krantz)

Published in: Time Magazine

Date: Oct 18, 1999

Source URL:
http://www.time.com/time/printout/0,8816,32207,00.html

252. Palo Alto Development

I live in Palo Alto, I moved there about ten years ago when I got
married and we had a child, because I wanted to be in more of a
community and have neighbours. The problem is that it's a nice
community, and a lot of people want to live there, and they're not
making any more Palo Alto. San Mateo's great, Burlingame's great,
San Carlos is great, all those towns are really good right now. But
they're getting discovered.

Name: Steve Jobs at 44 (Michael Krantz)

Published in: Time Magazine

Date: Oct 18, 1999

Source URL:
http://www.time.com/time/printout/0,8816,32207,00.html

253. Word 'Broadband

My personal belief is that you shouldn't use a word like broadband. It's this my terious thing. It's just fast networking, and I think people can understand that; high-speed networking vs. slower speed networking. I think this term broadband throws a lot of people off; they think it's something new and mysterious when all it is is their modem running 100 times faster.

Name: Steve Jobs at 44 (Michael Krantz)

Published in: Time Magazine

Date: Oct 18, 1999

Source URL:
http://www.time.com/time/printout/0,8816,32207,00.html

254. Reinventing Apple

One of the things that happened when we got back to Apple was, we said, Apple's all confused. Apple's forgotten what it is. Who is Apple? Why is Apple here? Remember, the roots of Apple were to build computers for people, not for corporations. At the time we started Apple, IBM built computers for corporations. Now it's Microsoft and Intel. But there was nobody building a computer for people. Funny enough, 20 years after we started Apple, there was nobody building computers for people again. You know? They were trying to sell consumers last year's corporate computers. We said, "Well, these are our roots. This is why we're here. The world doesn't need another Dell or Compaq. They need an Apple." We said, "Our thrust is not going to be to make computers for CEOs and enterprise companies." We have a lot of customers in the enterprise. But we don't ever go talk to the CEO of Time Warner. We talk to the people who put out the magazines.

Name: Steve Jobs at 44 (Michael Krantz)

Published in: Time Magazine

Date: Oct 18, 1999

Source URL:
http://www.time.com/time/printout/0,8816,32207,00.html

255. Art. Vs. Technology

I've never believed that they're separate. Leonardo da Vinci was a great artist and a great scientist. Michelangelo knew a tremendous amount about how to cut stone at the quarry. The finest dozen computer scientists I know are all musicians. Some are better than others, but they all consider that an important part of their life. I don't believe that the best people in any of these fields see themselves as one branch of a forked tree. I just don't see that. People bring these things together a lot. Dr. Land at Polaroid said, "I want Polaroid to stand at the intersection of art and science," and I've never forgotten that. I think that that's possible, and I think a lot of people have tried.

You said "corporate" and "technical" as if they go together. Technology has nothing to do with the corporate world. I don't see technology and the corporate world as being necessarily intertwined, any more than art and the corporate world are intertwined. Yes, I knew a lot of people when I was in my formative years who were very clear that they didn't want to grow up and work for some faceless corporation. They wanted to do something different with their lives, and a lot of them did. But that has nothing to do with science and technology and art. A lot of scientists have never worked in a corporation. And a lot of them started their own.

Name: Steve Jobs at 44 (Michael Krantz)

Published in: Time Magazine

Date: Oct 18, 1999

Source URL:
http://www.time.com/time/printout/0,8816,32207,00.html

256. Exciting Moment in History

It's a wonderful time right now. What we can put in a computer for $1000 is just mind blowing. We can use it to do wonderful things like video. It's pretty exciting right now. Apple is a large company, in a good sense. One of the reasons I came here was, when I was using NeXTStep, it was entropying. I didn't want to use the present state of Mac or Windows for the rest of my life. But another one was Apple had just lost a billion dollars. But what people forget is — someone once said that profit is the very small difference between two very large numbers: revenue and cost. Well, if Apple sold $7 billion worth of stuff, and it lost a billion, that means it spent $8 billion. That's a huge amount of money! It meant that this was a company that could spend $5, $6, $7 billion dollars a year and still make a profit! Which NeXT could not. If you could eliminate waste and work to come up with a focused strategy, you have enormous resources to do good work. It's a wonderful, wonderful opportunity.

Name: Steve Jobs at 44 (Michael Krantz)

Published in: Time Magazine

Date: Oct 18, 1999

Source URL:
http://www.time.com/time/printout/0,8816,32207,00.html

257. Changed As He Got Older

Sure, I mean people change. I get older. I'm a lot older. I'm 15 years older then when I left Apple. I left when I was 30. I'll be 45 in February. So, sure people change. When does your life really start as an adult? Lets say it starts when you're 15, you become totally conscious as an adult. So, I'm twice as old as an adult as when I was 30.

You know, I'm not sure it's always a good idea to chronicle one's point of view about oneself. I can tell you this: I've been married for 8 years, and that's had a really good influence on me. I've been very lucky, through random happenstance I just happened to sit next to this wonderful woman who became my wife. And it was a big deal. We have 3 kids, and it's been a big deal. You see the world differently. [When he came back to Apple] We had to lay some people off. A lot of people. I've done it before and it's always hard. But before, I didn't really think too much about it. But when I got here, every one that I had to do personally, I thought, "A lot of these fathers and mothers are going to have to go home and tell their families they just lost their jobs." And I'd never really thought about that before. You succeed at some things, you fail at some things. You start to understand what's important.

Name: Steve Jobs at 44 (Michael Krantz)

Published in: Time Magazine

Date: Oct 18, 1999

Source URL:
http://www.time.com/time/printout/0,8816,32207,00.html

258. Family Man

I've read something that Bill Gates said about six months ago. He said, "I worked really, really hard in my 20s." And I know what he means, because I worked really, really hard in my 20s too. Literally, you know, 7 days a week, a lot of hours every day. And it actually is a wonderful thing to do, because you can get a lot done. But you can't do it forever, and you don't want to do it forever, and you have to come up with ways of figuring out what the most important things are and working with other people even more. Just working smarter to get things done. Because you can't work 15 hour days, 7 days a week.

Name: Steve Jobs at 44 (Michael Krantz)

Published in: Time Magazine

Date: Oct 18, 1999

Source URL:
http://www.time.com/time/printout/0,8816,32207,00.html

259. Typical Workday

I'm a good morning person. I like it early in the morning. I wake up six-ish. About 10 years ago I put in a T1 to my house. I'm actually getting ready to put a 45 mg fiber to my house, because I want to find out what that will be like, because everybody's going to have that someday. But I have a pretty sophisticated set up; whether I'm at Apple or at Pixar or at my home, I log in and my whole world shows up on any of those computers. It's all kept on a server. So I carry none of it with me, but wherever I am, my complete world shows up, all my files. Everything. And I have high speed access to all of it. So my office is at home too. And when I'm not in meetings, my work is fundamentally on email. So I'll work a little before the kids get up. And then we'll all have a little food and finish up some homework and see them off to school. If I'm lucky I'll stay at home and work for an hour because I can get a lot done, but often times I'll have to come in. I usually get here about 9. 8 or 9. Having worked about an hour or half or two at home.

Name: Steve Jobs at 44 (Michael Krantz)

Published in: Time Magazine

Date: Oct 18, 1999

Source URL:
http://www.time.com/time/printout/0,8816,32207,00.html

260. His Job

Number one, everybody is compensated like a start up. Number two, we have a very simple, clear organisation. It's very easy to know who has authority for what, who has responsibility for what. There's no politics about it, they're virtually politics-free organisations. There's no turf wars. Avi runs software. John runs hardware. Mitch runs Sales. It's really simple. Number 3, we have a very simple mission. It's very easy to communicate what we're trying to do. I have a blast because I get to work with these super-talented people. Take Jony Ive. The last few weeks we've been working on this new product we're going to have a year from now. Just working out the concept for how it's gonna be. How we're going to engineer it, present it, what it's going to look like. We've had some incredible breakthroughs in a series of four or five hour-long conversations. Incredible breakthroughs. Our design group is light-years ahead of their peers.

Name: Steve Jobs at 44 (Michael Krantz)

Published in: Time Magazine

Date: Oct 18, 1999

Source URL:
http://www.time.com/time/printout/0,8816,32207,00.html

261. Answering Apple Email

Today's a slow day; I'll probably just have about 100 emails, Apple related. All these customers email me all these complaints and questions, which I actually have grown to like. It's like having a thermometer on practically any issue. If somebody doesn't flush a toilet around here, I get an email from Kansas about it. Sometimes I can get about 100 or more of those a day from people I will never meet. But I zing 'em around, and it's good to keep us all in touch.

Name: Steve Jobs at 44 (Michael Krantz)

Published in: Time Magazine

Date: Oct 18, 1999

Source URL:
http://www.time.com/time/printout/0,8816,32207,00.html

262. Hollywood and Silicon Valley

Hollywood's really different than Silicon Valley. And neither understands the other at all. People up here think being creative is some guys in their late 20s and early 30s sitting around old couches drinking beer thinking up jokes. It couldn't be further from the truth. The creative process is just as disciplined as the technical process; it requires just as much talent. And yet people in Hollywood think technology is only as deep as something you buy. There's no technical culture in Hollywood, they couldn't attract and retain good engineers to save their life, because they're second class citizens down there. Just like creative people are second class citizens in Silicon Valley.

Name: Steve Jobs at 44 (Michael Krantz)

Published in: Time Magazine

Date: Oct 18, 1999

Source URL:
http://www.time.com/time/printout/0,8816,32207,00.html

263. Object-oriented software

Objects are like people. They're living, breathing things that have knowledge inside them about how to do things and have memory inside them so they can remember things. And rather than interacting with them at a very low level, you interact with them at a very high level of abstraction, like we're doing right here. Here's an example: If I'm your laundry object, you can give me your dirty clothes and send me a message that says, "Can you get my clothes laundered, please." I happen to know where the best laundry place in San Francisco is. And I speak English, and I have dollars in my pockets. So I go out and hail a taxicab and tell the driver to take me to this place in San Francisco. I go get your clothes laundered, I jump back in the cab, I get back here. I give you your clean clothes and say, "Here are your clean clothes." You have no idea how I did that. You have no knowledge of the laundry place. Maybe you speak French, and you can't even hail a taxi. You can't pay for one, you don't have dollars in your pocket. Yet I knew how to do all of that. And you didn't have to know any of it. All that complexity was hidden inside of me, and we were able to interact at a very high level of abstraction. That's what objects are. They encapsulate complexity, and the interfaces to that complexity are high level.

Name: Steve Jobs in 1994 (Jeff Goodell)

Published in: Rolling Stone

Date: Jun 16, 199

Source URL: http://www.rollingstone.com/culture/news/steve-jobs-in-1994-the-rolling-stone-interview-20110117?print=true

264. Object-oriented operating system

They were working on the Mac for 10 years, too. I'm sure they're working on it. Microsoft's greatest asset is Windows. Their greatest liability is Windows. Windows is so non-object-oriented that it's going to be impossible for them to go back and become object-oriented without throwing Windows away, and they can't do that for years. So they're going to try to patch things on top, and it's not going to work.

Name: Steve Jobs in 1994 (Jeff Goodell)

Published in: Rolling Stone

Date: Jun 16, 199

Source URL: http://www.rollingstone.com/culture/news/steve-jobs-in-1994-the-rolling-stone-interview-20110117?print=true

265. Federal antitrust investigation

I don't have enough data to know. And again, the issue is not whether they accomplished what they did within the rule book or by breaking some of the rules. I'm not qualified to say. But I don't think it matters. I don't think that's the real issue. The real issue is, America is leading the world in software technology right now, and that is such a valuable asset for this country that anything that potentially threatens that leadership needs to be examined. I think the Microsoft monopoly of both sectors of the software industry — both the system and the applications software and the potential third sector that they want to monopolise, which is the consumer set-top-box sector — is going to pose the greatest threat to Americas dominance in the software industry of anything I have ever seen and could ever think of. I personally believe that it would be in the best interest of the country to break Microsoft up into three companies — a systems-software company, an applications-software company and a consumer-software company.

Name: Steve Jobs in 1994 (Jeff Goodell)

Published in: Rolling Stone

Date: Jun 16, 199

Source URL: http://www.rollingstone.com/culture/news/steve-jobs-in-1994-the-rolling-stone-interview-20110117?print=true

266. PowerPC

It works fine. It's a Pentium. The PowerPC and the Pentium are equivalent, plus or minus 10 or 20 percent, depending on which day you measure them. They're the same thing. So Apple has a Pentium. That's good. Is it three or four or five times better? No. Will it ever be? No. But it beats being behind.

Which was where the Motorola 68000 architecture was unfortunately being relegated. It keeps them at least equal, but it's not a compelling advantage.

Name: Steve Jobs in 1994 (Jeff Goodell)

Published in: Rolling Stone

Date: Jun 16, 199

Source URL: http://www.rollingstone.com/culture/news/steve-jobs-in-1994-the-rolling-stone-interview-20110117?print=true

267. Consumer research on the iMac

No. We have a lot of customers, and we have a lot of research into our installed base. We also watch industry trends pretty carefully. But in the end, for something this complicated, it's really hard to design products by focus groups. A lot of times, people don't know what they want until you show it to them. That's why a lot of people at Apple get paid a lot of money, because they're supposed to be on top of these things.

Name: Steve Jobs on Apple's resurgence (Andy Reinhardt)

Published in: Business Week

Date: May 12, 1998

Source URL: http://www.businessweek.com/bwdaily/dnflash/may1998/nf80512d.htm

268. Symbolic value

That's not my problem. I've worked my tail off here. I don't think I could work any harder. I'm trying to help Apple. I do have more time now to be with my family. We've filled out our senior management team. We've got a good team now, and we're firing on all cylinders. And as the strategy becomes clearer to more of the people in the company, it really makes things much easier. The organisation is clean and simple to understand, and very accountable. Everything just got simpler. That's been one of my mantras -- focus and simplicity. Simple can be harder than complex: You have to work hard to get your thinking clean to make it simple. But it's worth it in the end because once you get there, you can move mountains.

Name: Steve Jobs on Apple's resurgence (Andy Reinhardt)

Published in: Business Week

Date: May 12, 1998

Source URL:
http://www.businessweek.com/bwdaily/dnflash/may1998/nf80512d.htm

269. Sense of magic

You're missing it. This is not a one-man show. What's reinvigorating this company is two things: One, there's a lot of really talented people in this company who listened to the world tell them they were losers for a couple of years, and some of them were on the verge of starting to believe it themselves. But they're not losers. What they didn't have was a good set of coaches, a good plan. A good senior management team. They have that now. So, the first thing to invigorating people is winning again.

They're seeing us win, by the customer reactions to the products, by the sales, the profitability, all of those signs that people want what we've got again. That we can run our business well. That our own house is in order, that we've stopped the waste that people have seen with their own eyes without knowing what to do about it. There's sanity returning. The second thing that's reinvigorating them is that Apple is starting to innovate again. There's been a vacuum in this industry for a long time, in many ways, and that vacuum is in a lot of areas where Apple's legacy is. So Apple is back to its roots, starting to innovate again, and people are sensing that, seeing it concretely, and really feeling good about it. They came here. That's what they want to do. When they see the iMac, for example, they think we really can produce industry-leading products like this. It's not about charisma and personality, it's about results and products and those very bedrock things that are why people at Apple and outside of Apple are getting more excited about the company and what Apple stands for and what its potential is to contribute to the industry.

Name: Steve Jobs on Apple's resurgence (Andy Reinhardt)

Published in: Business Week

Date: May 12, 1998

Source URL:
http://www.businessweek.com/bwdaily/dnflash/may1998/nf80512d.htm

270. Why go legit

"Rip. Mix. Burn." was never not legit. When some folks thought "Rip. Mix. Burn." was an anthem to steal music, it was just because they didn't know what they were talking about. They obviously didn't have any kids living at home. This was the 50 year-old-crowd that thought that. We've been against stealing music since the beginning. We own a lot of intellectual property. Most of competitors don't, but we do. We're not happy when people steal. So, this is not an about face for us, or anything like that. We've been consistent from the beginning. "Rip. Mix. Burn." never meant go steal music—it meant rip, mix, burn—exactly what it said.

Name: Steve Jobs on the iTunes Music Store (Laura Locke)

Published in: Technologizer

Date: Apr 28, 2003

Source URL: http://technologizer.com/2011/12/07/steve-jobs-on-the-itunes-music-store-the-

unpublished-interview/

271. Music landscape

With the introduction of the new iTunes Music Store we've now built the first real complete ecosystem for the digital music age. We've got a way to buy music online legally that's fantastic—it's better than any other way to acquire music. We've got a way to manage music with the iTunes Jukebox, which is the best in the world. And we've got a way to listen to music on the go with the iPod—which is the most popular MP3 player in the world—and the coolest, one of the coolest things in the world. So we've really got, from one end to another, a complete solution for digital music. We're the only people in the world to do this, so we feel great about it.

Name: Steve Jobs on the iTunes Music Store (Laura Locke)

Published in: Technologizer

Date: Apr 28, 2003

272. Digital music impresario

I didn't know what it meant. Does that mean I run a carnival? What we do at Apple is very simple: we invent stuff. We make the best personal computers in the world, some of the best software, the best portable MP3/music player, and now we make the best online music store in the world. We just make stuff. So I don't know what impresario means. We make stuff, put it out there, and people use it. Clearly, we've been leading the revolution. The personal computer is changing—it's changing into this digital hub for a digital lifestyle—so we've been leading that change, we're not followers, we've lead that charge. Digital movie making, DVD burning, digital photography, and of course, digital music. So we are in the forefront.

Name: Steve Jobs on the iTunes Music Store (Laura Locke)

Published in: Technologizer

Date: Apr 28, 2003

273. Music Store's development costs or Apple's investment

Well, we don't usually talk about that, but all I would say is that... you know I had somebody comment today, "Well, now that you have introduced your store, do you expect a lot others?" And I guess our answer is no. This is really hard. Just to create an infrastructure to pump oceans of bits out in the world, you know, we've done that over the last several years with movie trailers and stuff, and that's tens of millions of dollars for server farms and networking farms – it's huge – and we've already got that in place, and say you want to have millions of transactions, and our online store is all tied into SAP and auditors bless it, and to do that, that's tens of millions of dollars, and we have one-click shopping, and only us and Amazon have that, and then to make a jukebox, if you don't a popular jukebox, how much does it cost to make iTunes and make it popular? A lot! But we've got that. And then iPod, if you want to make an iPod, what does that cost? Well, nobody has done it but us, people have tried, but they haven't even come close. That's a lot of money. So we've already made these investments and we can leverage all these investments. And then we've invested more on top of that to make a store. But to recreate this, it's tens of millions of dollars and years. That's why I don't think this is going to be so easy to copy.

Name: Steve Jobs on the iTunes Music Store (Laura Locke)

Published in: Technologizer

Date: Apr 28, 2003

Source URL: http://technologizer.com/2011/12/07/steve-jobs-on-the-itunes-music-store-the-

unpublished-interview/

274. Sell your music service concept to music industry executives

Well, we started almost a year and a half ago, and as you recall, the climate at that time was more hostile than it is today, but we did have the luxury of going in at the top, so I talked to Roger Aims at Warner, Doug Morris at Universal, and the other guys. And they clearly realised that the Internet was in their future, but they were shell-shocked with Napster and people stealing their content. And so, the major discussions with the labels were really over giving the users broad personal use rights. And we worked through that, and they learned. I think they trusted us to do the right thing. You know most everybody in the music industry uses a Mac—and they all have iPods—even the ones who don't use a computer have somebody else load up their iPods for 'em with the songs they want. So I think they see Apple as the most creative of the technical companies, a very artist-friendly company, very credible. And you know, we were able to negotiate landmark deals with them that no one else has ever come close to in terms of offering the user really broad rights to the music they buy.

Name: Steve Jobs on the iTunes Music Store (Laura Locke)

Published in: Technologizer

Date: Apr 28, 2003

Source URL: http://technologizer.com/2011/12/07/steve-jobs-on-the-itunes-music-store-the-

unpublished-interview/

275. Independent labels

Yes. They've already been calling us like crazy. We've had to put most of them off until after launch just because the major big five have most of the music, and we only had so many hours in the day. But now we're really going to have time to focus on a lot of the independents and that will be really great.

Name: Steve Jobs on the iTunes Music Store (Laura Locke)

Published in: Technologizer

Date: Apr 28, 2003

Source URL: http://technologizer.com/2011/12/07/steve-jobs-on-the-itunes-music-store-the-

unpublished-interview/

276. Parallel between the music and the PC

Obviously, the biggest difference is that this time we're on Windows. Other than that, I'm not so sure. It's still very early in the music revolution. Remember, there are 10 billion songs that are distributed in the U.S. every year – legally – on CDs. So far on iTunes, we've distributed about 16 million [as of October]. So we're at the very beginning of this.

Name: Steve Jobs: Rolling Stone's 2003 Interview (Jeff Goodell)

Published in: Rolling Stone

Date: Dec 25, 2003

Source URL: http://www.rollingstone.com/music/news/steve-jobs-rolling-stones-2003-interview-20111006

277. Companies react on board with Apple

There are a lot of smart people at the music companies. The problem is they're not technology people. The good music companies do an amazing thing. They have people who can pick the person who's gonna be successful out of 5,000 candidates. It's an intuitive process. And the best music companies know how to do that with a reasonably high success rate. I think that's a good thing. The world needs more smart editorial these days. The problem is that that has nothing to do with technology. When the Internet came along and Napster came along, people in the music business didn't know what to make of the changes. A lot of these folks didn't use computers, weren't on e-mail – didn't really know what Napster was for a few years. They were pretty dog gone slow to react. Matter of fact, they still haven't really reacted. So they're vulnerable to people telling them technical solutions will work – when they won't.

Name: Steve Jobs: Rolling Stone's 2003 Interview (Jeff Goodell)

Published in: Rolling Stone

Date: Dec 25, 2003

Source URL: http://www.rollingstone.com/music/news/steve-jobs-rolling-stones-2003-interview-20111006

278. Clone

I'd answer that by saying I think Amazon does pretty well against Microsoft. So does eBay. So does Google. And AOL has actually done pretty well, too – contrary to a lot of the things people say. There are a lot of examples of companies offering services, Internet-based services, that have done quite well. And Apple is in a pretty interesting position. Because, as you may know, almost every song and

CD is made on a Mac – it's recorded on a Mac, it's mixed on a Mac, the artwork's done on a Mac. Almost every artist I've met has an iPod, and most of the music execs now have iPods. And one of the reasons Apple was able to do what we have done was because we are perceived by the music industry as the most creative technology company. And now we've created this music store, which I think is non-trivial to copy. I mean, to say that Microsoft can just decide to copy it, and copy it in six months – that's a big statement. It may not be so easy.

Name: Steve Jobs: Rolling Stone's 2003 Interview (Jeff Goodell)

Published in: Rolling Stone

Date: Dec 25, 2003

Source URL: http://www.rollingstone.com/music/news/steve-jobs-rolling-stones-2003-interview-20111006

279. Birth of the iPhone

"We all had cellphones. We just hated them, they were so awful to use. The software was terrible. The hardware wasn't very good. We talked to our friends, and they all hated their cellphones too. Everybody seemed to hate their phones. And we saw that these things really could become much more powerful and interesting to license. It's a huge market. I mean a billion phones get shipped every year, and that's almost an order of magnitude greater than the number of music players. It's four times the number of PCs that ship every year. "It was a great challenge. Let's make a great phone that we fall in love with. And we've got the technology. We've got the miniaturisation from the iPod. We've got the sophisticated operating system from Mac. Nobody had ever thought about putting operating systems as sophisticated as OS X inside a phone, so that was a real question. We had a big debate inside the company whether we could do that or not. And that was one where I had to adjudicate it and just say, 'We're going to do it. Let's try.' The smartest software guys were saying they can do it, so let's give them a shot. And they did."

Name: Steve Jobs Speaks Out (Betsy Morris)

Published in: Fortune

Date: Feb 2008

Source URL:
http://money.cnn.com/galleries/2008/fortune/0803/gallery.jobsqna.fortune/index.html

280. Choosing strategy

"We do no market research. We don't hire consultants. The only consultants I've ever hired in my 10 years is one firm to analyse Gateway's retail strategy so I would not make some of the same mistakes they made [when launching Apple's retail stores]. But we never hire consultants, person. We just want to make great products. "When we created the iTunes Music Store, we did that because we thought it would be great to be able to buy music electronically, not because we had plans to redefine the music industry. I mean, it just seemed like writing on the wall, that eventually all music would be distributed electronically. That seemed obvious because why have the cost? The music industry has huge returns. Why have all this [overhead] when you can just send electrons around easily?"

Name: Steve Jobs Speaks Out (Betsy Morris)

Published in: Fortune

Date: Feb 2008

281. Apple employees

"We don't get a chance to do that many things, and every one should be really excellent. Because this is our life. Life is brief, and then you die, you know? So this is what we've chosen to do with our life. We could be sitting in a monastery somewhere in Japan. We could be out sailing. Some of the [executive team] could be playing golf. They could be running other companies. And we've all chosen to do this with our lives. So it better be damn good. It better be worth it. And we think it is."

Name: Steve Jobs Speaks Out (Betsy Morris)

Published in: Fortune

Date: Feb 2008

282. People want to work at Apple

"The reason is, is because you can't do what you can do at Apple anywhere else. The engineering is long gone in most PC companies. In the consumer electronics companies, they don't understand the software parts of it. And so you really can't make the products that you can make at Apple anywhere else right now. Apple's the only company that has everything under one roof. "There's no other

203

company that could make a MacBook Air and the reason is that not only do we control the hardware, but we control the operating system. And it is the intimate interaction between the operating system and the hardware that allows us to do that. There is no intimate interaction between Windows and a Dell notebook. "Our DNA is as a consumer company -- for that individual customer who's voting thumbs up or thumbs down. That's who we think about. And we think that our job is to take responsibility for the complete user experience. And if it's not up to par, it's our fault, plain and simply."

Name: Steve Jobs Speaks Out (Betsy Morris)

Published in: Fortune

Date: Feb 2008

Source URL:
http://money.cnn.com/galleries/2008/fortune/0803/gallery.jobsqna.fortune/index.html

283. Apple's focus

"Apple is a $30 billion company, yet we've got less than 30 major products. I don't know if that's ever been done before. Certainly the great consumer electronics companies of the past had thousands of products. We tend to focus much more. People think focus means saying yes to the thing you've got to focus on. But that's not what it means at all. It means saying no to the hundred other good ideas that there are. You have to pick carefully. "I'm actually as proud of many of the things we haven't done as the things we have done. The clearest example was when we were pressured for years to do a PDA, and I realised one day that 90% of the people who use a PDA only take information out of it on the road. They don't put information into it. Pretty soon cellphones are going to do that, so the PDA market's going to get reduced to a fraction of its current size, and it won't really be sustainable. So we decided not to get into it. If we had gotten into it, we wouldn't have had the resources to do the iPod. We probably wouldn't have seen it coming."

Name: Steve Jobs Speaks Out (Betsy Morris)

Published in: Fortune

Date: Feb 2008

Source URL:
http://money.cnn.com/galleries/2008/fortune/0803/gallery.jobsqna.fortune/index.html

284. Management style

"We've got 25,000 people at Apple. About 10,000 of them are in the stores. And my job is to work with sort of the top 100 people, that's what I do. That doesn't mean they're all vice presidents. Some of them are just key individual contributors. So when a good idea comes, you know, part of my job is to move it around, just see what different people think, get people talking about it, argue with people about it, get ideas moving among that group of 100 people, get different people together to explore different aspects of it quietly, and, you know - just explore things."

Name: Steve Jobs Speaks Out (Betsy Morris)

Published in: Fortune

Date: Feb 2008

Source URL:
http://money.cnn.com/galleries/2008/fortune/0803/gallery.jobsqna.fortune/index.html

285. Finding talent

"When I hire somebody really senior, competence is the ante. They have to be really smart. But the real issue for me is, Are they going to fall in love with Apple? Because if they fall in love with Apple, everything else will take care of itself. They'll want to do what's best for Apple, not what's best for them, what's best for Steve, or anybody else. "Recruiting is hard. It's just finding the needles in the haystack. We do it ourselves and we spend a lot of time at it. I've participated in the hiring of maybe 5,000-plus people in my life. So I take it very seriously. You can't know enough in a one-hour interview. So, in the end, it's ultimately based on your gut. How do I feel about this person? What are they like when they're challenged? Why are they here? I ask everybody that: 'Why are you here?' The answers themselves are not what you're looking for. It's the meta-data."

Name: Steve Jobs Speaks Out (Betsy Morris)

Published in: Fortune

Date: Feb 2008

Source URL:
http://money.cnn.com/galleries/2008/fortune/0803/gallery.jobsqna.fo
rtune/index.html

286. Benefits of owning an operating system

"That allows us to innovate at a much faster rate than if we had to wait for Microsoft, like Dell and HP and everybody else does. Because Microsoft has their own timetable, for probably good reasons. I mean Vista took what — seven or eight years? It's hard to get your new feature that you need for your new hardware if it has to wait eight years. So we can set our own priorities and look at things in a more holistic way from the point of view of the customer. It also means that we can take it and we can make a version of it to fit in the iPhone and the iPod. And, you know, we certainly couldn't do that if we didn't own it."

Name: Steve Jobs Speaks Out (Betsy Morris)

Published in: Fortune

Date: Feb 2008

Source URL:
http://money.cnn.com/galleries/2008/fortune/0803/gallery.jobsqna.fo
rtune/index.html

287. Marathon Monday meetings

"When you hire really good people you have to give them a piece of the business and let them run with it. That doesn't mean I don't get to kibitz a lot. But the reason you're hiring them is because you're going to give them the reins. I want [them] making as good or better decisions than I would. So the way to do that is to have them know everything, not just in their part of the business, but in every part of the business. "So what we do every Monday is we review the whole business. We look at what we sold the week before. We look at every single product under development, products we're having trouble with, products where the demand is larger than we can make. All the stuff in development, we review. And we do it every single week. I put out an agenda -- 80% is the same as it was the last week, and we just walk down it every single week. "We don't have a lot of process at Apple, but that's one of the few things we do just to all stay on the same page."

Name: Steve Jobs Speaks Out (Betsy Morris)

Published in: Fortune

Date: Feb 2008

Source URL:
http://money.cnn.com/galleries/2008/fortune/0803/gallery.jobsqna.fortune/index.html

288. Roadblocks

"At Pixar when we were making Toy Story, there came a time when we were forced to admit that the story wasn't great. It just wasn't great. We stopped production for five months.... We paid them all to twiddle their thumbs while the team perfected the story into what became Toy Story. And if they hadn't had the courage to stop, there would have never been a Toy Story the way it is, and there probably would have never been a Pixar. "We called that the 'story crisis,' and we never expected to have another one. But you know what? There's been one on every film. We don't stop production for five months. We've gotten a little smarter about it. But there always seems to come a moment where it's just not working, and it's so easy to fool yourself - to convince yourself that it is when you know in your heart that it isn't. "Well, you know what? It's been that way with [almost] every major project at Apple, too....

Name: Steve Jobs Speaks Out (Betsy Morris)

Published in: Fortune

Date: Feb 2008

Source URL:
http://money.cnn.com/galleries/2008/fortune/0803/gallery.jobsqna.fortune/index.html

289. iPod tipping point

"It was difficult for a while because for various reasons the Mac had not been accepted by a lot of people, who went with Windows. And we were just working really hard, and our market share wasn't going up. It makes you wonder sometimes whether you're wrong. Maybe our stuff isn't better, although we thought it was. Or maybe people don't care, which is even more depressing. "It turns out with the iPod we kind of got out from that operating-system glass ceiling and it was great because [it showed that] Apple innovation, Apple engineering, Apple design did matter. The iPod captured 70% market share. I cannot tell you how important that was after so many years of labouring and seeing a 4% to 5% market share on the Mac. To see something like that happen with the iPod was a great shot in the arm for everybody."

Name: Steve Jobs Speaks Out (Betsy Morris)

Published in: Fortune

Date: Feb 2008

Source URL:
http://money.cnn.com/galleries/2008/fortune/0803/gallery.jobsqna.fortune/index.html

290. Launching the Apple store

"It was very simple. The Mac faithful will drive to a destination, right? They'll drive somewhere special just to do that. But people who own Windows - we want to convert them to Mac. They will not drive somewhere special. They don't think they want a Mac. They will not take the risk of a 20-minute drive in case they don't like it. "But if we put our store in a mall or on a street that they're walking by, and we reduce that risk from a 20-minute drive to 20 footsteps, then they're more likely to go in because there's really no risk. So we decided to put our stores in high-traffic locations. And it works."

Name: Steve Jobs Speaks Out (Betsy Morris)

Published in: Fortune

Date: Feb 2008

Source URL:
http://money.cnn.com/galleries/2008/fortune/0803/gallery.jobsqna.fortune/index.html

291. Managing through the economic downturn

"We've had one of these before, when the dot-com bubble burst. What I told our company was that we were just going to invest our way through the downturn, that we weren't going to lay off people, that we'd taken a tremendous amount of effort to get them into Apple in the first place -- the last thing we were going to do is lay them off. And we were going to keep funding. In fact we were going to up our R&D budget so that we would be ahead of our competitors when the downturn was over. And that's exactly what we did. And it worked. And that's exactly what we'll do this time."

Name: Steve Jobs Speaks Out (Betsy Morris)

Published in: Fortune

Date: Feb 2008

Source URL:
http://money.cnn.com/galleries/2008/fortune/0803/gallery.jobsqna.fortune/index.html